Solving Math Problems and Summarizing Results

BY
DON BLATTNER AND MYRL SHIREMAN

COPYRIGHT © 2005 Mark Twain Media, Inc.

ISBN 1-58037-319-4

Printing No. D04003

Mark Twain Media, Inc., Publishers
Distributed by Carson-Dellosa Publishing Company, Inc.

Revised/Original title: *Understanding Math Through Writing and Reading*

Table of Contents

Introduction

The criticism of schools heard most often is that students are not learning the basics. "The basics," that people generally refer to are the three R's: 'readin', 'riten' and 'rithmetic. They often point to specific instances they have witnessed where graduates were unable to demonstrate basic skills that should have been mastered in school. While much of the criticism can be dismissed as unjustified or just a nostalgic wish to return to a simpler, happier time, these critics can't be ignored. The instances they claim to have witnessed are often true.

Does this mean that teachers aren't doing their job or that students are not working to master these skills? Not at all. What it does mean is that students sometimes have difficulty transferring the skills they have learned in school into real life situations. For example, students usually master the formula for figuring the area of a rectangle quite easily. The teacher explains the formula and gives a number of problems to reinforce the concept. Most students are able to work the problems quickly and progress to more difficult mathematical challenges. A few years later when they graduate, their employer may say, "I need this room painted. Figure out how much paint we need and go buy it." The young man shrugs and asks, "How do I do that?" He was unable to make the connection between the problems he found so easy in school and the real problem that he was now asked to solve.

As educators we must help students understand that the facts, formulas, and procedures that are taught in school are only a part of their mathematical education. They need to be able to use these facts, formulas, and procedures in order to apply them to new situations they will encounter once they graduate. Students must learn that understanding how a problem is solved is as important as the answer.

This is no easy task. We have learned, though, that if students are given an opportunity to become actively involved with mathematics by reading, writing, describing, and explaining mathematical concepts, they not only understand these concepts better, they are able to transfer the concepts to new problems. Writing is not just a basic skill important for communication, it is also a learning tool.

The connection between writing and mathematics should not come as a surprise to teachers. Writing is the use of symbols to express ideas and relationships. Mathematics is the use of symbols to express quantities and relationships. When we strengthen one skill, we also strengthen the other.

The purpose of this book is twofold. *First, students will use writing as a tool to improve their understanding of mathematics.* By reading, writing, explaining, illustrating, and discussing mathematical concepts, students will develop a better understanding of these concepts and they will also have the opportunity to incorporate mathematics into their world. *Second, students will use mathematics in order to develop and utilize their writing skills.* Their comprehension, reasoning, organizational, and sequencing skills will be challenged and strengthened.

Name _____ Date _____

Writing to Understand the Rule

In the following exercises, you are to be a detective. You will be given the name of a specific kind of problem. The name of the problem will indicate what you are supposed to do in order to solve the problem. However, you will *not* be given any instructions as to how this problem or similar problems are to be solved. Instead, you will be shown several completed examples of the problem. From these examples you should be able to understand what the problem is all about and how to solve similar problems. You will be able to check out your understanding by solving additional problems. Your final task is to write a rule that will help others work out problems of this type.

CHANGING FRACTIONS TO HIGHER TERMS

When someone changes a fraction to higher terms, they form more, but smaller parts.

Example: $\frac{1}{2} = ?$

$$\frac{1}{2} = \frac{1 \times 2}{2 \times 2} = \frac{2}{4} \quad \text{or} \quad \frac{1}{2} = \frac{1 \times 3}{2 \times 3} = \frac{3}{6} \quad \text{or} \quad \frac{1}{2} = \frac{1 \times 4}{2 \times 4} = \frac{4}{8} \quad \text{or} \quad \frac{1}{2} = \frac{1 \times 5}{2 \times 5} = \frac{5}{10}$$

$$\frac{1}{2} = \frac{1 \times 6}{2 \times 6} = \frac{6}{12} \quad \text{or} \quad \frac{1}{2} = \frac{1 \times 7}{2 \times 7} = \frac{7}{14} \quad \text{or} \quad \frac{1}{2} = \frac{1 \times 8}{2 \times 8} = \frac{8}{16} \quad \text{or} \quad \frac{1}{2} = \frac{1 \times 9}{2 \times 9} = \frac{9}{18}$$

EXERCISE A

Change these fractions to higher terms:

1. $\frac{1}{3}$ 2. $\frac{3}{4}$ 3. $\frac{4}{5}$

The following example will show you how you are to complete this kind of problem and how to fill in the blanks on similar "Writing to Understand the Rule" exercises.

1. $\frac{1}{3} = \frac{1 \times 2}{3 \times 2} = \frac{2}{6}$ 2. $\frac{3}{4} = \frac{3 \times 2}{4 \times 2} = \frac{6}{8}$ 3. $\frac{4}{5} = \frac{4 \times 2}{5 \times 2} = \frac{8}{10}$

What did you do to work these problems?

I found in order to change a fraction to a higher term, all that I have to do is to multiply both terms (numerator and denominator) of the fraction by the same number. I can multiply by any number as long as I remember to multiply both terms by that same number.

State this understanding in the form of a mathematical rule so that others will be able to read the rule and work similar problems.

Rule to Change Fractions to Higher Terms:

If both terms of a fraction are multiplied by the same number, the value of the fraction remains the same.

Name _____ Date _____

Writing to Understand the Rule

You will *not* be given any instructions as to how the following problems are to be solved. Instead, you will be shown several completed examples, and from these examples you should be able to understand what the problem is all about and how to solve similar problems. You will be able to check out your understanding by solving additional problems. Your final task is to write a rule that will help others work out problems of this type.

REDUCING TO COMMON FRACTIONS

When someone reduces a fraction, they reduce that fraction to fewer, but larger, parts.

Examples

$$\frac{4}{8} \div \frac{4}{4} = \frac{1}{2} \qquad \frac{2}{16} \div \frac{2}{2} = \frac{1}{8} \qquad \frac{75}{100} \div \frac{25}{25} = \frac{3}{4}$$

EXERCISE 1

Reduce these problems:

1. $\frac{3}{6}$ 　　　　　 2. $\frac{4}{6}$ 　　　　　 3. $\frac{4}{20}$ 　　　　　 4. $\frac{4}{16}$

5. $\frac{8}{12}$ 　　　　　 6. $\frac{3}{12}$ 　　　　　 7. $\frac{32}{64}$ 　　　　　 8. $\frac{6}{8}$

9. $\frac{9}{24}$ 　　　　 10. $\frac{18}{60}$ 　　　　 11. $\frac{12}{15}$ 　　　　 12. $\frac{12}{16}$

13. $\frac{4}{4}$ 　　　　 14. $\frac{10}{14}$ 　　　　 15. $\frac{30}{36}$

What did you do to work these problems? _____

_____

_____

_____

State this understanding in the form of a mathematical rule so that others will be able to read the rule and work similar problems.

Rule to Reduce to Common Fractions: _____

_____

_____

_____

Name _____ Date _____

Writing to Understand the Rule

You will *not* be given any instructions as to how the following problems are to be solved. Instead, you will be shown several completed examples, and from these examples you should be able to understand what the problem is all about and how to solve similar problems. You will be able to check out your understanding by solving additional problems. Your final task is to write a rule that will help others work out problems of this type.

ADDING OR SUBTRACTING FRACTIONS WITH THE SAME DENOMINATOR

In order to be added or subtracted, fractions must have like denominators.

Examples

$$\frac{2}{4} + \frac{1}{4} = \frac{3}{4} \qquad \frac{2}{5} + \frac{1}{5} = \frac{3}{5} \qquad \frac{4}{12} + \frac{3}{12} = \frac{7}{12}$$

$$\frac{2}{4} - \frac{1}{4} = \frac{1}{4} \qquad \frac{2}{5} - \frac{1}{5} = \frac{1}{5} \qquad \frac{4}{12} - \frac{3}{12} = \frac{1}{12}$$

EXERCISE 2

Work these problems:

1. $\frac{3}{6} + \frac{2}{6} =$ 2. $\frac{3}{20} + \frac{4}{20} =$ 3. $\frac{9}{24} + \frac{5}{24} =$

4. $\frac{4}{16} + \frac{12}{16} =$ 5. $\frac{8}{12} + \frac{3}{12} =$ 6. $\frac{32}{64} + \frac{3}{64} =$

7. $\frac{7}{20} - \frac{4}{20} =$ 8. $\frac{3}{4} + \frac{1}{4} =$ 9. $\frac{5}{14} + \frac{3}{14} =$

10. $\frac{6}{9} - \frac{2}{9} =$ 11. $\frac{17}{50} - \frac{8}{50} =$ 12. $\frac{11}{25} - \frac{3}{25} =$

What did you do to work these problems? _____

_____

_____

_____

State this understanding in the form of a mathematical rule so that others will be able to read the rule and work similar problems.

Rule to Add or Subtract Fractions With the Same Denominator: _____

_____

_____

Name_____ Date _____

Writing to Understand the Rule

You will *not* be given any instructions as to how the following problems are to be solved. Instead, you will be shown several completed examples, and from these examples you should be able to understand what the problem is all about and how to solve similar problems. You will be able to check out your understanding by solving additional problems. Your final task is to write a rule that will help others work out problems of this type.

ADDING OR SUBTRACTING FRACTIONS WITH DIFFERENT DENOMINATORS

In order to be added or subtracted, fractions must have like denominators.

Examples

$$\frac{1}{2} = \frac{2}{4} \qquad \frac{1}{3} = \frac{2}{6} \qquad \frac{1}{5} = \frac{3}{15} \qquad \frac{1}{2} = \frac{5}{10}$$

$$+\frac{1}{4} = \frac{1}{4} \qquad +\frac{2}{6} = \frac{2}{6} \qquad +\frac{3}{15} = \frac{3}{15} \qquad +\frac{7}{10} = \frac{7}{10}$$

$$\frac{3}{4} \qquad\qquad \frac{4}{6} \qquad\qquad \frac{6}{15} \qquad\qquad \frac{12}{10} = 1\frac{1}{5}$$

EXERCISE 3

Work these problems:

1. $\frac{3}{5} + \frac{2}{12} =$ 2. $\frac{3}{20} + \frac{4}{10} =$ 3. $\frac{9}{16} + \frac{5}{4} =$ 4. $\frac{4}{16} + \frac{12}{32} =$

5. $\frac{8}{9} + \frac{3}{12} =$ 6. $\frac{1}{2} + \frac{3}{18} =$ 7. $\frac{7}{10} - \frac{4}{20} =$ 8. $\frac{3}{4} + \frac{1}{8} =$

9. $\frac{5}{14} + \frac{3}{7} =$ 10. $\frac{6}{9} - \frac{2}{36} =$ 11. $\frac{17}{50} - \frac{8}{100} =$ 12. $\frac{10}{25} - \frac{15}{50} =$

What did you do to work these problems? _____

_____

_____

State this understanding in the form of a mathematical rule so that others will be able to read the rule and work similar problems.

Rule for Adding or Subtracting Fractions With Different Denominators: _____

_____

_____

Name _____ Date _____

Writing to Understand the Rule

You will *not* be given any instructions as to how the following problems are to be solved. Instead, you will be shown several completed examples, and from these examples you should be able to understand what the problem is all about and how to solve similar problems. You will be able to check out your understanding by solving additional problems. Your final task is to write a rule that will help others work out problems of this type.

MULTIPLYING FRACTIONS

Examples

$$\frac{1}{2} \times \frac{2}{3} = \frac{2}{6} = \frac{1}{3} \qquad \frac{3}{8} \times \frac{2}{3} = \frac{6}{24} = \frac{1}{4} \qquad \frac{1}{5} \times \frac{3}{6} = \frac{3}{30} = \frac{1}{10}$$

EXERCISE 4

Work these problems:

1. $\frac{3}{6} \times \frac{2}{12} =$ 2. $\frac{3}{20} \times \frac{4}{10} =$ 3. $\frac{9}{16} \times \frac{5}{4} =$

4. $\frac{4}{16} \times \frac{12}{32} =$ 5. $\frac{8}{9} \times \frac{3}{12} =$ 6. $\frac{30}{64} \times \frac{3}{18} =$

7. $\frac{7}{10} \times \frac{4}{20} =$ 8. $\frac{3}{4} \times \frac{1}{8} =$ 9. $\frac{5}{14} \times \frac{3}{7} =$

10. $\frac{6}{9} \times \frac{2}{32} =$ 11. $\frac{17}{50} \times \frac{8}{100} =$ 12. $\frac{10}{25} \times \frac{15}{50} =$

What did you do to work these problems? _____

_____

_____

_____

State this understanding in the form of a mathematical rule so that others will be able to read the rule and work similar problems.

Rule for Multiplying Fractions: _____

_____

_____

_____

_____

Name_____ Date_____

Writing to Understand the Rule

You will *not* be given any instructions as to how the following problems are to be solved. Instead, you will be shown several completed examples, and from these examples you should be able to understand what the problem is all about and how to solve similar problems. You will be able to check out your understanding by solving additional problems. Your final task is to write a rule that will help others work out problems of this type.

MULTIPLYING A FRACTION AND A WHOLE NUMBER

Examples

$$3 \times \frac{2}{3} = \frac{3 \times 2}{3} = \frac{6}{3} = 2 \qquad\qquad 5 \times \frac{6}{9} = \frac{5 \times 6}{9} = \frac{30}{9} = 3\frac{1}{3}$$

$$4 \times \frac{1}{8} = \frac{4 \times 1}{8} = \frac{4}{8} = \frac{1}{2} \qquad\qquad 7 \times \frac{9}{10} = \frac{7 \times 9}{10} = \frac{63}{10} = 6\frac{3}{10}$$

EXERCISE 5

Work these problems:

1. $2 \times \frac{2}{3} =$ 2. $3 \times \frac{5}{10} =$ 3. $\frac{5}{16} \times 8 =$

4. $\frac{1}{2} \times 10 =$ 5. $9 \times \frac{5}{12} =$ 6. $212 \times \frac{3}{9} =$

7. $70 \times \frac{4}{21} =$ 8. $34 \times \frac{3}{18} =$ 9. $314 \times \frac{15}{18} =$

10. $\frac{6}{9} \times 32 =$ 11. $50 \times \frac{8}{100} =$ 12. $1025 \times \frac{35}{50} =$

What did you do to work these problems? _____

_____

_____

_____

State this understanding in the form of a mathematical rule so that others will be able to read the rule and work similar problems.

Rule for Multiplying a Fraction and a Whole Number: _____

_____

_____

_____

Name _____ Date _____

Writing to Understand the Rule

You will *not* be given any instructions as to how the following problems are to be solved. Instead, you will be shown several completed examples, and from these examples you should be able to understand what the problem is all about and how to solve similar problems. You will be able to check out your understanding by solving additional problems. Your final task is to write a rule that will help others work out problems of this type.

MULTIPLYING FRACTIONS AND MIXED NUMBERS

Examples

$$3\frac{1}{2} \times \frac{2}{3} = \frac{7}{2} \times \frac{2}{3} = \frac{14}{6} = 2\frac{1}{3}$$

$$49\frac{16}{32} \times \frac{4}{9} = \frac{1584}{32} \times \frac{4}{9} = \frac{6336}{288} = 22$$

$$12\frac{2}{3} \times \frac{3}{4} = \frac{38}{3} \times \frac{3}{4} = \frac{114}{12} = 9\frac{1}{2}$$

$$4\frac{1}{4} \times \frac{1}{8} = \frac{17}{4} \times \frac{1}{8} = \frac{17}{32}$$

EXERCISE 6

Work these problems:

1. $4 \times 1\frac{7}{8} =$

2. $2\frac{1}{3} \times \frac{2}{6} =$

3. $7\frac{1}{2} \times \frac{3}{5} =$

4. $\frac{1}{2} \times 9\frac{1}{8} =$

5. $50\frac{2}{3} \times \frac{3}{5} =$

6. $42\frac{1}{4} \times \frac{1}{6} =$

7. $24\frac{1}{5} \times \frac{4}{5} =$

8. $21\frac{1}{3} \times \frac{2}{3} =$

9. $3\frac{1}{4} \times 3\frac{1}{4} =$

10. $3\frac{1}{2} \times 3\frac{4}{3} =$

11. $3\frac{1}{4} \times 2\frac{5}{16} =$

12. $5\frac{1}{2} \times 3\frac{1}{2} =$

What did you do to work these problems? _____

_____

State this understanding in the form of a mathematical rule so that others will be able to read the rule and work similar problems.

Rule for Multiplying Fractions and Mixed Numbers: _____

_____

_____

Name _____ Date _____

Writing to Understand the Rule

You will *not* be given any instructions as to how the following problems are to be solved. Instead, you will be shown several completed examples, and from these examples you should be able to understand what the problem is all about and how to solve similar problems. You will be able to check out your understanding by solving additional problems. Your final task is to write a rule that will help others work out problems of this type.

DIVIDING FRACTIONS

Examples

$$\frac{3}{4} \div \frac{2}{3} = \frac{3}{4} \times \frac{3}{2} = \frac{9}{8} = 1\frac{1}{8} \qquad \frac{1}{2} \div \frac{1}{2} = \frac{1}{2} \times \frac{2}{1} = \frac{2}{2} = 1$$

$$\frac{1}{8} \div \frac{1}{4} = \frac{1}{8} \times \frac{4}{1} = \frac{4}{8} = \frac{1}{2} \qquad \frac{1}{5} \div \frac{1}{10} = \frac{1}{5} \times \frac{10}{1} = \frac{10}{5} = 2$$

EXERCISE 7

Work these problems:

1. $\frac{1}{6} \div \frac{7}{8} =$ 2. $\frac{1}{3} \div \frac{5}{6} =$ 3. $\frac{1}{2} \div \frac{3}{5} =$

4. $\frac{1}{2} \div \frac{1}{3} =$ 5. $\frac{3}{5} \div \frac{3}{5} =$ 6. $\frac{7}{5} \div \frac{1}{6} =$

7. $\frac{5}{13} \div \frac{4}{5} =$ 8. $\frac{5}{9} \div \frac{2}{3} =$ 9. $\frac{1}{4} \div \frac{1}{9} =$

10. $\frac{1}{2} \div \frac{4}{3} =$ 11. $\frac{1}{8} \div \frac{5}{16} =$ 12. $\frac{9}{2} \div \frac{1}{2} =$

What did you do to work these problems? _____

_____

_____

_____

State this understanding in the form of a mathematical rule so that others will be able to read the rule and work similar problems.

Rule for Dividing Fractions: _____

_____

_____

Name_____ Date_____

Writing to Understand the Rule

You will *not* be given any instructions as to how the following problems are to be solved. Instead, you will be shown several completed examples, and from these examples you should be able to understand what the problem is all about and how to solve similar problems. You will be able to check out your understanding by solving additional problems. Your final task is to write a rule that will help others work out problems of this type.

DIVIDING MIXED NUMBERS OR A FRACTION BY WHOLE NUMBERS

Examples

$$3\frac{2}{3} \div \frac{3}{4} = \frac{11}{3} \times \frac{4}{3} = \frac{44}{9} = 4\frac{8}{9} \qquad 5 \div \frac{3}{4} = \frac{5}{1} \times \frac{4}{3} = \frac{20}{3} = 6\frac{2}{3}$$

$$9\frac{1}{4} \div \frac{1}{8} = \frac{37}{4} \times \frac{8}{1} = \frac{296}{4} = 74 \qquad 6\frac{1}{2} \div 5\frac{1}{3} = \frac{13}{2} \times \frac{3}{16} = \frac{39}{32} = 1\frac{7}{32}$$

EXERCISE 8

Work these problems:

1. $9\frac{1}{6} \div \frac{7}{8} =$

2. $13 \div \frac{1}{3} =$

3. $7\frac{1}{2} \div 6\frac{3}{5} =$

4. $9\frac{1}{2} \div 3\frac{1}{3} =$

5. $5\frac{3}{4} \div \frac{3}{5} =$

6. $2 \div \frac{1}{8} =$

7. $16 \div \frac{2}{3} =$

8. $90 \div \frac{5}{9} =$

9. $6\frac{1}{14} \div 2\frac{1}{9} =$

10. $8\frac{1}{2} \div 8\frac{1}{2} =$

11. $11\frac{1}{8} \div \frac{5}{16} =$

12. $150 \div 12\frac{1}{2} =$

What did you do to work these problems? _____

_____

_____

_____

State this understanding in the form of a mathematical rule so that others will be able to read the rule and work similar problems.

Rule for Dividing Mixed Numbers or a Fraction By Whole Numbers: _____

_____

_____

_____

Name _____ Date _____

Writing to Understand the Rule

You will *not* be given any instructions as to how the following problems are to be solved. Instead, you will be shown several completed examples, and from these examples you should be able to understand what the problem is all about and how to solve similar problems. You will be able to check out your understanding by solving additional problems. Your final task is to write a rule that will help others work out problems of this type.

EXPRESSING COMMON FRACTIONS AS DECIMALS

Examples

$$\frac{1}{2} = 2\overline{)1.0} \quad \frac{0.5}{}$$
$$\frac{10}{0}$$
$\frac{1}{2} = 0.5$

$$\frac{3}{4} = 4\overline{)3.00} \quad \frac{0.75}{}$$
$$\frac{28}{20}$$
$$\frac{20}{0}$$
$\frac{3}{4} = 0.75$

$$\frac{3}{8} = 8\overline{)3.000} \quad \frac{0.375}{}$$
$$\frac{24}{60}$$
$$\frac{56}{40}$$
$$\frac{40}{0}$$
$\frac{3}{8} = 0.375$

EXERCISE 9

Work these problems:

1. $\frac{8}{16} =$ 2. $\frac{3}{36} =$ 3. $\frac{7}{12} =$ 4. $\frac{9}{12} =$ 5. $\frac{3}{5} =$ 6. $\frac{1}{8} =$

7. $\frac{2}{3} =$ 8. $\frac{5}{9} =$ 9. $\frac{1}{4} =$ 10. $\frac{3}{8} =$ 11. $\frac{5}{16} =$ 12. $\frac{2}{9} =$

What did you do to work these problems? _____

_____

State this understanding in the form of a mathematical rule so that others will be able to read the rule and work similar problems.

Rule for Expressing Common Fractions as Decimals: _____

_____

Name _____ Date _____

Writing to Understand the Rule

You will *not* be given any instructions as to how the following problems are to be solved. Instead, you will be shown several completed examples, and from these examples you should be able to understand what the problem is all about and how to solve similar problems. You will be able to check out your understanding by solving additional problems. Your final task is to write a rule that will help others work out problems of this type.

DIVIDING DECIMALS AND PLACING THE DECIMAL

Examples

$$0.8\overline{)4} \qquad 0.02\overline{)5} \qquad 0.0023\overline{)69}$$

$$0.8 \times 10\overline{)4 \times 10} \qquad 0.02 \times 100\overline{)5 \times 100} \qquad 0.0023 \times 10{,}000\overline{)69 \times 10{,}000}$$

$$
\begin{array}{r}
5 \\
8\overline{)40} \\
\underline{40} \\
0
\end{array}
\qquad
\begin{array}{r}
250 \\
2\overline{)500} \\
\underline{4} \\
10 \\
\underline{10} \\
0\ 0 \\
\underline{0} \\
0
\end{array}
\qquad
\begin{array}{r}
30{,}000 \\
23\overline{)690{,}000} \\
\underline{69} \\
00 \\
\underline{0} \\
00 \\
\underline{0} \\
00 \\
\underline{0} \\
00 \\
\underline{0} \\
0
\end{array}
$$

EXERCISE 10

Work these problems:

1. $1.9\overline{)38}$ 2. $0.7\overline{)125}$ 3. $0.03\overline{)39.75}$ 4. $0.009\overline{)0.5625}$ 5. $0.0013\overline{)1.3}$

What did you do to work these problems? _____

_____

State this understanding in the form of a mathematical rule so that others will be able to read the rule and work similar problems.

Rule for Dividing Decimals and Placing the Decimal: _____

_____

Name _____ Date _____

Writing to Understand the Rule

You will *not* be given any instructions as to how the following problems are to be solved. Instead, you will be shown several completed examples, and from these examples you should be able to understand what the problem is all about and how to solve similar problems. You will be able to check out your understanding by solving additional problems. Your final task is to write a rule that will help others work out problems of this type.

MULTIPLYING AND PLACING THE DECIMAL

Examples

7	0.7	0.07	0.007	0.0007	0.00007	0.07	0.0007
x 5	x 5	x 5	x 5	x 5	x 0.05	x 0.05	x 0.05
35	3.5	0.35	0.035	0.0035	0.0000035	0.0035	0.000035

EXERCISE 11

Work these problems:

1. 0.09
    x 0.9

2.   31
    x 0.02

3.   120
    x 0.6

4.   5.89
    x 0.33

5.   506
    x 0.01

6.   230
    x 0.005

7.   58
    x 0.04

8. 0.015
    x 1.5

What did you do to work these problems? _____

_____

_____

State this understanding in the form of a mathematical rule so that others will be able to read the rule and work similar problems.

Rule for Multiplying and Placing the Decimal: _____

_____

_____

Name_____ Date_____

Writing to Understand the Rule

You will *not* be given any instructions as to how the following problems are to be solved. Instead, you will be shown several completed examples, and from these examples you should be able to understand what the problem is all about and how to solve similar problems. You will be able to check out your understanding by solving additional problems. Your final task is to write a rule that will help others work out problems of this type.

MULTIPLYING AND DIVIDING BY 10, 100, AND 1000

Examples

3.8 x 10 = 38	3.8 x 100 = 380	3.8 x 1000 = 3800	0.380 x 100 = 38
3.8 ÷ 10 = 0.38	3.8 ÷ 100 = 0.038	3.8 ÷ 1000 = 0.0038	0.38 ÷100 = 0.0038

EXERCISE 12

Multiply by 10	1. 49 _____	2. 3.6 _____	3. 0.02 _____	4. 98 _____
Multiply by 100	5. 39 _____	6. 2.3 _____	7. 0.05 _____	8. 89 _____
Multiply by 1000	9. 5 _____	10. 5.9 _____	11. 0.07 _____	12. 27 _____
Divide by 10	13. 18 _____	14. 6.9 _____	15. 0.08 _____	16. 13 _____
Divide by 100	17. 67 _____	18. 7.1 _____	19. 0.05 _____	20. 41 _____
Divide by 1000	21. 87 _____	22. 4.3 _____	23. 0.09 _____	24. 57 _____

Rules for Multiplying and Dividing by 10, 100, and 1000:

25. To multiply a decimal by 10, I moved the decimal point_____ places to the _____.

26. To multiply a decimal by 100, I moved the decimal point _____ places to the _____.

27. To multiply a decimal by 1000, I moved the decimal point _____ places to the _____.

28. To divide a decimal by 10, I moved the decimal point _____ places to the _____.

20. To divide a decimal by 100, I moved the decimal point _____ places to the _____.

30. To divide a decimal by 1000, I moved the decimal point _____ places to the _____.

Name _____ Date _____

Create a Test

The class has been studying adding, subtracting, multiplying, and dividing whole numbers, fractions, and decimals. Your assignment is to make a test that covers all of the concepts covered:

- Reducing to Common Fractions

- Adding or Subtracting Fractions With the Same Denominator

- Adding or Subtracting Fractions With Different Denominators

- Multiplying a Fraction

- Multiplying a Fraction and a Whole Number

- Multiplying Fractions and Mixed Numbers

- Dividing Fractions

- Dividing Mixed Numbers or Fractions By Whole Numbers

- Expressing Common Fractions as Decimals

- Dividing Decimals

- Multiplying and Placing the Decimal

- Multiplying and Dividing by 10, 100, and 1000

Your test should have at least 20 problem-type questions such as $1/4 \div 1/2 =$ ___. It should also include at least five story or word problems. However, you do not need to limit yourself to these kinds of problems. If you choose, you may create matching, true-false, multiple choice, word search, crossword puzzle, or any other type of problem you think would be appropriate to include in a test.

Make sure you not only create the test, but that you work the problems so that you have an answer key.

Name _____   Date _____

Writing to Understand the Rule

You will *not* be given any instructions as to how the following problems are to be solved. Instead, you will be shown several completed examples, and from these examples you should be able to understand what the problem is all about and how to solve similar problems. You will be able to check out your understanding by solving additional problems. Your final task is to write a rule that will help others work out problems of this type.

EQUATIONS

Solving an equation when the variable is multiplied by a number.

Examples

$$2x = 14$$
$$\frac{2x}{2} = \frac{14}{2}$$
$$x = 7$$

$$4x = 12$$
$$\frac{4x}{4} = \frac{12}{4}$$
$$x = 3$$

$$12x = 36$$
$$\frac{12x}{12} = \frac{36}{12}$$
$$x = 3$$

$$8x = 48$$
$$\frac{8x}{8} = \frac{48}{8}$$
$$x = 6$$

EXERCISE 13

Work these problems.

1. $4x = 24$ 2. $11x = 33$ 3. $9x = 72$ 4. $7x = 56$

5. $1.8x = 9$ 6. $4.5x = 18$ 7. $4x = 24$ 8. $18.4x = 92$

What did you do to work these problems? _____

_____

_____

State this understanding in the form of a mathematical rule so that others will be able to read the rule and work similar problems.

Rule for solving an equation when the variable is multiplied by a number: _____

_____

_____

Name _____ Date _____

Writing to Understand the Rule

You will *not* be given any instructions as to how the following problems are to be solved. Instead, you will be shown several completed examples, and from these examples you should be able to understand what the problem is all about and how to solve similar problems. You will be able to check out your understanding by solving additional problems. Your final task is to write a rule that will help others work out problems of this type.

EQUATIONS

Solving an equation when the variable is divided by a number.

Examples

$$\frac{x}{3} = 18 \qquad \frac{x}{10} = 2 \qquad \frac{x}{11} = 2 \qquad \frac{x}{28} = 2.9$$

$$\frac{1}{\cancel{3}} \cdot \frac{x}{\cancel{3}_1} = 18 \cdot 3 \quad \frac{1}{\cancel{10}} \cdot \frac{x}{\cancel{10}_1} = 2 \cdot 10 \quad \frac{1}{\cancel{11}} \cdot \frac{x}{\cancel{11}_1} = 2 \cdot 11 \quad \frac{1}{\cancel{28}} \cdot \frac{x}{\cancel{28}_1} = 2.9 \cdot 28$$

$$x = 54 \qquad x = 20 \qquad x = 22 \qquad x = 81.2$$

EXERCISE 14

Solve these problems.

1. $\dfrac{x}{4} = 48$

2. $\dfrac{x}{24} = 96$

3. $\dfrac{x}{8} = 48$

4. $\dfrac{x}{3} = 0.08$

5. $\dfrac{x}{9} = 4.5$

6. $\dfrac{x}{1.8} = 0.98$

7. $\dfrac{x}{1.08} = 37$

8. $\dfrac{x}{11} = 99$

What did you do to work these problems? _____

_____

_____

State this understanding in the form of a mathematical rule so that others will be able to read the rule and work similar problems.

Rule for solving an equation when the variable is divided by a number: _____

_____

_____

Name _____ Date _____

Writing to Understand the Rule
USING INVERSE OPERATIONS

You can solve equations by doing **inverse operations**. Do you know what the word *inverse* means? Write the definition below. If you are not sure of the exact meaning of the word, look it up in the dictionary.

Inverse: _____

_____

EXERCISE 15

Write the inverse operation for each of the following terms

TERM	INVERSE OPERATION IS
Addition	1. _____
Subtraction	2. _____
Multiplication	3. _____
Division	4. _____

Solve the problems listed below using the inverse operation rule. To the right of the problem, explain what you did and why.

Explanation

5. $x + 2 = 36$ 5. _____

6. $x - 6 = 98$ 6. _____

7. $9x = 24$ 7. _____

8. $\dfrac{x}{0.2} = 3.8$ 8. _____

Name_____ Date _____

Writing to Understand Plane Figures

The figure to the left is a square. The size of this square can be measured in two ways. You can measure the distance around the square in order to find the **perimeter**, or you can measure the **area** inside the square. The units for the two types of measurement are different.

MEASURING THE PERIMETER AND AREA OF SQUARES AND RECTANGLES
EXERCISE 16

Measure the square with a ruler. What is the perimeter of the square? (1) _____
What is the area? (2) _____. Your answer reflects the different ways of expressing the two kinds of measurement. We call these two units of measure **linear measure** and **area measure**.

The first column of the following chart lists the linear measure. Opposite each unit, write the area measure.

Linear Measure	Area Measure
Inch	3. _____
Foot	4. _____
Yard	5. _____
Millimeter	6. _____
Centimeter	7. _____
Decimeter	8. _____
Meter	9. _____
Mile	10. _____
Hectare	11. _____

Using a straight edge, connect the points A to B to D to C to A in order to make a square and points G to E to F to H to G in order to make a rectangle.

FIGURE 1   **FIGURE 2**

A•   •B   E•   •F

C•   •D   G•   •H

Name_____ Date _____

EXERCISE 16 (CONTINUED)

FIGURE 1

In order to complete the exercise, you must understand how to bisect. Do you know what the word *bisect* means? Write the definition below. If you are not sure of the exact meaning of the word, look it up in the dictionary.

12. Bisect:_____

Now complete the following steps for Figure 1.

- Bisect line AB. (Place a dot at the midpoint on line AB.)
- Bisect line CD. (Place a dot at the midpoint on line CD.)
- With a straight edge, draw a line connecting these two points.
- Bisect line AC. (Place a dot at the midpoint on line AC.)
- Bisect line BD. (Place a dot at the midpoint on line BD.)
- With a straight edge, draw a line connecting these two points.

13. Describe Figure 1 now that you have drawn the lines. _____

_____

_____

14. Using a ruler, measure the perimeter of Figure 1. _____

15. Without measuring, can you determine the area of Figure 1? If so, what is it? _____
    Use a ruler to check your guess.

FIGURE 2

Now complete the following steps for Figure 2.

- On line EF, measure one inch to the right from point E and place a dot there.
- On line GH, measure one inch to the right from point G and place a dot there.
- With a straight edge, draw a line connecting these two points.
- On line EF, measure one inch to the left from point F and place a dot there.
- On line GH, measure one inch to the left from point H and place a dot there.
- With a straight edge, draw a line connecting these two points.
- Bisect line EG. (Place a dot at the midpoint on line EG.)
- Bisect line FH. (Place a dot at the midpoint on line FH.)
- With a straight edge, draw a line connecting these two points.

16. Describe Figure 2 now that you have drawn the lines: _____

_____

_____

Name _____ Date _____

17. Using a ruler, measure the perimeter of the figure. _____

18. Without measuring, can you determine the area of the figure? _____
    If so, what is it? _____ Use a ruler to check your guess.

    You have just determined the perimeter and the area of these two figures **directly**. In the blank below, write the definition for measuring directly.

19. Direct Measurement: _____

    There is another way, however, to measure area. It is called **indirect** measurement. When you use indirect measurement, you are able to find the area by using the **length** and **width** of a square of a rectangle.
    Look at Figure 1 and Figure 2. Can you discover what formula you would use in order to find the area of these two plane figures?

20. Write the formula for figuring area of a square and a rectangle. _____

In your own words, explain what the formula means. _____

_____

    Use this formula to figure the area of the following squares whose sides are:

21. 4 cm _____ 22. 9 mm _____ 23. 12.5 in _____ 24. 17 yd _____

25. 1.3 ft _____ 26. 4.6 mi _____ 27. 32.90 m _____ 28. 18.7 ft _____

    Figure the area of the following rectangles whose dimensions are:

29. L = 2 in. W = 4 in _____   30. L = 8.5 in W = 2 in _____

31. L = 4 yds. W = 4 yds _____   32. L = 12 yds W = 14 yds _____

33. L = 2.7 mm W = 4 mm _____   34. L = 8.1 yds W = 4 yds _____

35. L = 4.7miles W = 2.3 mi _____ 36. L = 3 cm W = 8 cm _____

Name_____ Date_____

EXERCISE 17: FINDING THE PERIMETER AND AREA OF FIGURES

Find the perimeter and the area of the following figures. Write the steps you took in order to find the answers to the right of the figures.

Figure 1

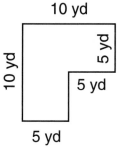

Figure 2

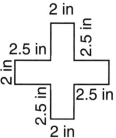

Figure 3

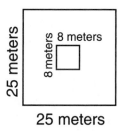

Figure 4

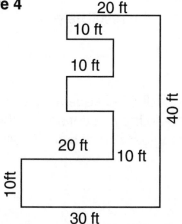

1. Perimeter: _____

_____

2. Area: _____

_____

_____

_____

3. Perimeter: _____

_____

4. Area: _____

_____

_____

_____

5. Perimeter of outside figure: _____

_____

_____

6. Area of outside figure minus area of inside figure:

_____

_____

_____

_____

7. Perimeter: _____

_____

_____

_____

8. Area: _____

_____

_____

_____

_____

Name _____ Date _____

MEASURING THE AREA OF A TRIANGLE
EXERCISE 18

Using a straight edge, connect the points A to B to D to C to A in order to make a square and points E to F to H to G to E in order to make a rectangle.

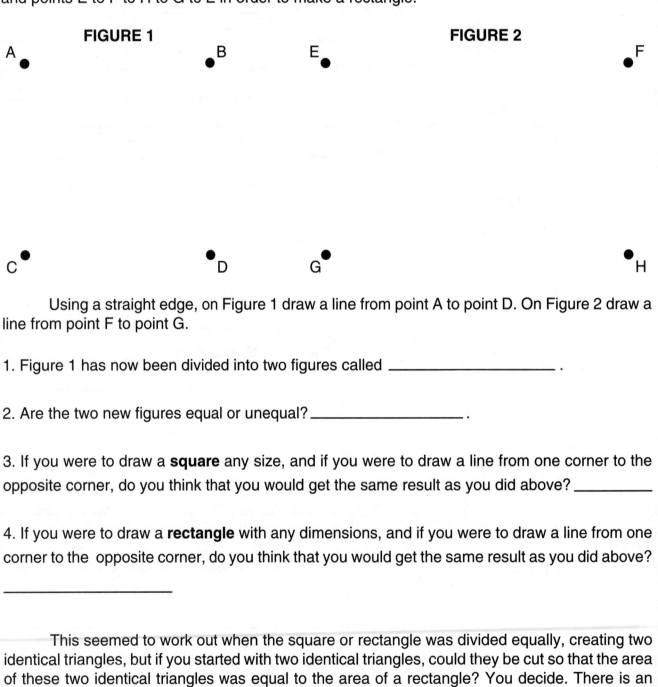

FIGURE 1   **FIGURE 2**

A   B   E   F

C   D   G   H

Using a straight edge, on Figure 1 draw a line from point A to point D. On Figure 2 draw a line from point F to point G.

1. Figure 1 has now been divided into two figures called _____ .

2. Are the two new figures equal or unequal? _____ .

3. If you were to draw a **square** any size, and if you were to draw a line from one corner to the opposite corner, do you think that you would get the same result as you did above? _____

4. If you were to draw a **rectangle** with any dimensions, and if you were to draw a line from one corner to the opposite corner, do you think that you would get the same result as you did above?

_____

This seemed to work out when the square or rectangle was divided equally, creating two identical triangles, but if you started with two identical triangles, could they be cut so that the area of these two identical triangles was equal to the area of a rectangle? You decide. There is an example on the next page demonstrating this principle.

Name _____ Date _____

EXERCISE 18 (CONTINUED)

Draw two identical triangles.

Divide one triangle into two other triangles.

Invert the two smaller triangles and place them together.

Place the two smaller triangles over one of the original triangles.

5. What figure is formed? _____

6. What is the formula for figuring the area of this figure? _____

7. In your own words, what does this tell you about the area of a triangle as compared to the area of a square or a rectangle? _____

_____

You know that in order to find the area of a square or of a rectangle you use the formula **length x width equals area (A = l x w)**. Given what you have just discovered, what would you guess the formula to find the area of a triangle would be?

8. Write a formula for determining the area of a triangle. _____

After you have written the formula, check in your math book to see if it is correct.

Name _____ Date _____

FINDING THE AREA OF A TRIANGLE
EXERCISE 19

     It is important to understand the terms used when figuring the area of a triangle. For a square or a rectangle, the terms **length** and **width** are used. These terms are easy to understand and to use. The dimensions of a triangle aren't as apparent as they are with a square or a rectangle. The terms are different as well. When figuring the area of a triangle, the terms **base** and **height** are used. The base of a triangle is any side of the triangle. The height of the triangle is the perpendicular distance from the vertex (the highest point) opposite the base of the triangle. The height is **not** the dimensions of any of the sides. Here are some examples.

Figure 1   **Figure 2**   **Figure 3**

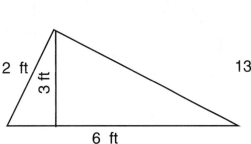
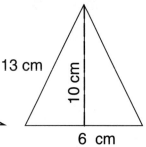
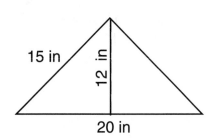

1. In Figure 1, the dimension of the base is _____ and the dimension of the height is _____ .

2. In Figure 2, the dimension of the base is _____ and the dimension of the height is _____ .

3. In Figure 3, the dimension of the base is _____ and the dimension of the height is _____ .

     Use the formula you have devised to figure the area of triangles with the following dimensions. You will be given dimensions for the base (b) and the height (h).

4. b = 7, h = 5 _____   5. b = 6, h = 25 _____

6. b = 3, h = 2 _____   7. b = 7.2, h = 5.1 _____

8. b = 25, h = 7.6 _____   9. b = 34.25, h = 12 _____

10. b = 17.2, h = 13.2 _____   11. b = 137.5, h = 11.2 _____

12. b = $3\frac{1}{2}$, h = $\frac{1}{2}$ _____   13. b = $9\frac{3}{4}$, h = $2\frac{1}{2}$ _____

14. b = $11\frac{2}{3}$, h = 9 _____   15. b = $11\frac{1}{8}$, h = $11\frac{1}{6}$ _____

16. b = $9\frac{1}{72}$, h = $2\frac{3}{18}$ _____   17. b = $3\frac{1}{9}$, h = $5\frac{1}{36}$ _____

Name_____   Date_____

EXERCISE 20: LEARNING MORE ABOUT TRIANGLES

Look at Figure A below and see how many geometric forms you can identify or make by using the parts labeled "a," "b," and "c." Place a plus (+) on the blank for Questions 1 through 4 if you find the geometric form in Figure A.

Figure A

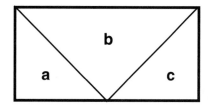

_____ 1. A right triangle   _____ 2. A square   _____ 3. A rectangle   _____ 4. A parallelogram

5. On your own paper write a description of a figure like Figure A, but with a width of two inches and a length of four inches. Give your description to a friend and see if he or she can accurately draw the new figure using only your written description.

Figure B below is the same as Figure A except that the dashed line divides the figure into parts "a," "b," "c," and "d." Refer to Figure B and answer the following questions.

Figure B

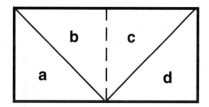

6. There are _____ triangles in Figure B.

7. There are _____ squares in Figure B.

8. There are _____ right triangles in Figure B.

9. The area of "a" and "b" together is _____ square inch(es).

10. The area of "c" and "d" together is _____ square inch(es).

11. The area of "b" and "c" together is _____ square inch(es).

12. The area of "a" and "d" together is _____ square inch(es).

13. Part "a" is what fractional part of Figure B? _____

14. Part "b" is what fractional part of Figure B? _____

15. Part "c" is what fractional part of Figure B? _____

16. Part "d" is what fractional part of Figure B? _____

17. Does "a" + "b" equal "c" + "d"? _____

18. Does "a" + "d" equal "b" + "c"? _____

Name _____ Date _____

EXERCISE 20: LEARNING MORE ABOUT TRIANGLES (CONTINUED)

19. In the space below redraw (reposition) parts "a," "b," "c," and "d" so that the figure is in the shape of a perfect square. Label the parts in the square.

20. On your own paper write a description of a figure like Figure B, but with a width of two inches and a length of four inches. Give your description to a friend and see if the friend can accurately draw the new figure using only your written description.

21. Figure C at right is a rectangle with the same length and width as Figures A and B. Divide the rectangle into four equal rectangles and eight right triangles. Begin dividing Figure C by connecting points "a" and "b." Next, connect points "c" and "d." Then continue on your own.

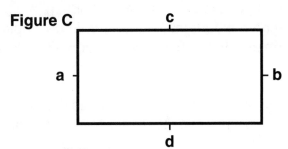
Figure C

22. Figure D at right is a rectangle with the same length and width as Figure C. Divide the rectangle into four equal rectangles and eight right triangles. You **cannot** draw line "a—b" as you did in Figure C.

Figure D

23. Figure E at right is a rectangle with the same width as Figures C and D. Divide Figure E into eight right triangles. You must draw lines "a—b" and "c—d" last on Figure E.

        Refer to Figures C, D, and E and answer the following questions.

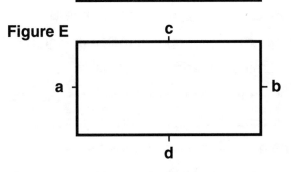
Figure E

24. The area of each of the rectangles in Figure C is _____ square inches.

25. The area of each of the right triangles in Figure C is _____ square inches.

26. The area of each of the rectangles in Figure D is _____ square inches.

27. The area of each of the right triangles in Figure D is _____ square inches.

28. The area of each of the rectangles in Figure E is _____ square inches.

29. The area of each of the right triangles in Figure E is _____ square inches.

Name_____ Date_____

MEASURING THE AREA OF A PARALLELOGRAM
EXERCISE 21

In previous lessons you learned the formula for finding the area of a square or rectangle is
(1) _____ . You have also learned the formula for finding the area of a triangle is
(2) _____ . Now we are going to study **parallelograms**.

Write the definition of a parallelogram. If you don't know the definition and you are unable to figure out the meaning from the name, look up the definition in a dictionary or math book.

3. Parallelogram: _____

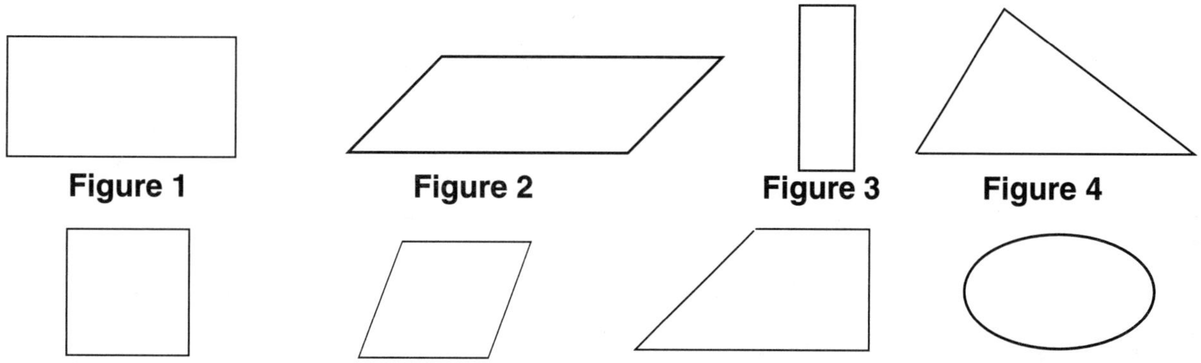

Figure 1   **Figure 2**   **Figure 3**   **Figure 4**

Figure 5   **Figure 6**   **Figure 7**   **Figure 8**

4. Which of the above figures are parallelograms? _____
5. What are the names of those figures that are not parallelograms? _____
_____

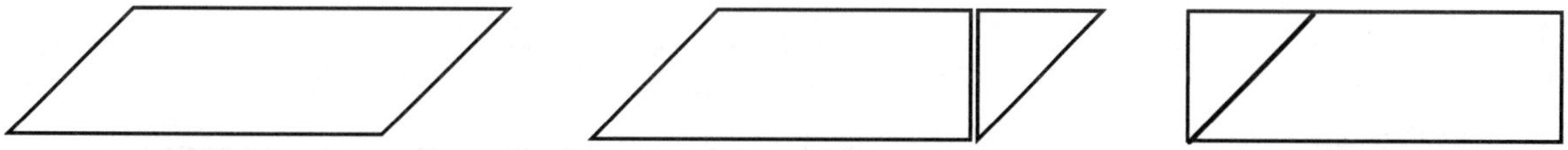

Step 1   **Step 2**   **Step 3**

6. Look at the parallelogram in Step 1. See how it can easily be converted into another figure? What is the name of this figure that it can be converted into? _____
7. Is the area of the original parallelogram in Step 1 more than, less than, or the same as the area in the final figure in Step 3? _____
8. What is the formula for the area of the figure in Step 3? _____
9. What would you guess the formula for area to be for the figure in Step 1 (parallelogram)? Write the formula for area for a parallelogram. Check the formula in your math book to see if your answer is correct. _____

Name _____   Date _____

EXERCISE 21 (CONTINUED)

As with a triangle, the height of a parallelogram is not as easy to determine as it is in a square or rectangle. When figuring the area of a parallelogram, the terms **base** and **height** are used. The base of the parallelogram is obvious, but the height is not. **The height of a parellogram is the perpendicular distance between the base and the side opposite the base. The height is not the dimensions of any of the sides as it is in a square or rectangle. Here is an example.**

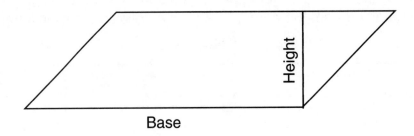

Base

10. b = 8, h = 6 _____

11. b = 7, h = 24 _____

12. b = 2, h = 2 _____

13. b = 7.1, h = 3.2 _____

14. b = 23, h = 6.6 _____

15. b = 31.15, h = 10 _____

16. b = 13.5, h = 14.2 _____

17. b = 107.5, h = 23.2 _____

18. b = $5\frac{1}{3}$, h = $\frac{2}{3}$ _____

19. b = $8\frac{1}{4}$, h = $2\frac{1}{8}$ _____

20. b = $33\frac{1}{6}$, h = 9 _____

21. b = $15\frac{1}{4}$, h = $11\frac{2}{16}$ _____

22. b = $6\frac{1}{36}$, h = $5\frac{3}{9}$ _____

23. b = $2\frac{1}{18}$, h = $3\frac{3}{72}$ _____

Name _____ Date _____

MEASURING THE AREA OF A CIRCLE

In the circle below, **C** stands for **circumference**, the distance around the circle; **r** represents **radius**, a line that joins the center of a circle with any point on its circumference; and **d** means **diameter**, a straight line passing through the center of a circle, ending at the circumference.

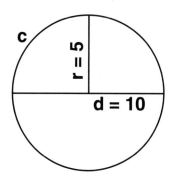

EXERCISE 22

Look around your home and find twelve items that are circular, such as the lid to a jar, the top of a can, or a coaster.

- List these items on the chart below in the Item column.
- Measure the circumference of each item, and record the dimensions on the chart in the Circumference column.
- Measure the diameter of each item, and record the dimensions on the chart in the Diameter column.
- Divide the circumference by the diameter, and record the result in the Unknown column.
- Find the average for the Unknown column.
- Compare your average to the average of the other students in class.
- If possible, find an average for the class.

Item	Circumference	Diameter	Unknown

Name _____   Date _____

EXERCISE 22 (CONTINUED)

1. What is the average of your Unknown column? _____

2. What do you think this represents? _____

Your answer for problem #1 should be approximately 3.14. If it is not, it is probably because the measuring device you used is not accurate. The figure 3.14 represents the value of π (pi). **Pi** (π) is the symbol for the ratio of the circumference of a circle to its diameter. Pi, or 3.14159…, is an **irrational number** and cannot be expressed as a terminating decimal number. It can be carried out to millions of digits past the decimal. For most purposes, the figure 3.1416 is accurate enough. If you need to express π in the form of a fraction, it is $\frac{22}{7}$.

3. You were able to find the value of pi by dividing the circumference of a circle by the diameter. If you only knew the circumference of a circle, how would you find the diameter of a circle?

_____

Find the diameters of the following circles. The circumferences are given. Use 3.14 for π.

4. 6 cm _____   5. 17 in. _____   6. 32 m _____   7. 18 mm _____

8. 12 yds. _____   9. 23.47 ft. _____   10. 13.01 miles _____   11. 312.8 m _____

12. How would you find the circumference of an object if you knew only the diameter?

_____

Find the circumferences of the following circles. The diameters are given. Use 3.14 for π.

13. 3 cm _____   14. 13 in. _____   15. 23 m _____   16. 12 mm _____

17. 9 yds. _____   18. 13.07 ft. _____   19. 213 miles _____   20. 110.7 m _____

21. How would you find the circumference of an object if you knew only the radius?

_____

Find the circumference of the following circles. The radii of the circles are given. Use 3.14 for π.

22. 2 cm _____   23. 28 in. _____   24. 7.2 m _____   25. 7.13 mm _____

26. 7 yds. _____   27. 17.07 ft. _____   28. 6.12 miles_____   29. 123.8 m _____

30. Based on the problems you have just worked, write the formula to find the diameter of a circle when you only know the circle's circumference:

d = _____

31. Write the formula to find the circumference of a circle when you only know the circle's diameter:

c = _____

32. Write the formula to find the circumference of a circle when you only know the circle's radius:

c = _____

Name _____ Date _____

EXERCISE 22 (CONTINUED)

To find the area of a circle, use this formula: $A = \pi r^2$. Here are the steps you go through to find the area of a circle whose radius is 2.4:

$A = \pi r^2$
$A = 3.14 \times 2.4^2$
$A = 3.14 \times (2.4 \times 2.4)$
$A = 18.09$

Find the areas of the circles with the following radii:

33. 22 cm _____ 34. 79 in. _____ 35. 13 m _____ 36. 23mm _____
37. 11 yds. _____ 38. 13.43 ft. _____ 39. 9.56 miles _____ 40. 110.8 m _____

EXERCISE 23: WRITING TO UNDERSTAND THE MATH

You are a pen pal with a young girl from Ecuador who is just beginning to study circles in her math class at school. In a letter she asks you to explain how to figure the area of a circle. Write her a letter discussing the terms **circumference**, **diameter**, **radius**, and **pi**. Explain how to figure the area of a circle. Since her English is limited, your explanation will need to be very simple and easy to understand. You may, of course, use diagrams.

_____
_____
_____
_____
_____
_____
_____
_____
_____
_____
_____

Name _____ Date _____

Below is a circle with a dot locating the center. Refer to this circle and answer the following questions.

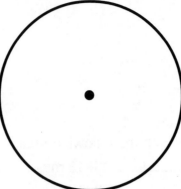

Fill in the blank and circle the appropriate answer.

1. The diameter of the circle is (a) _____ (b) inches / square inches.

2. The radius of the circle is (a) _____ (b) inches / square inches.

3. The circumference of the circle is (a) _____ (b) inches / square inches.

4. The area of the circle is (a) _____ (b) inches / square inches.

Draw a square over the above circle with each side two inches long. The circle will then be completely inside the square with the edge of the circle touching each of the four sides of the square but not overlapping.

5. The perimeter of the square is (a) _____ (b) inches / square inches.

6. The area of the square is (a) _____ (b) inches / square inches.

7. Write what you know about the circle. _____

_____

8. Write what you know about the square. _____

_____

9. Write how the circle and the square are alike. _____

_____

What Do You Think?

10. If you double the size of the diameter of the circle, will the area double?   yes/no

11. If you double the size of the diameter of the circle, will the circumference double?   yes/no

12. If you double the length of the sides of the square, will the area double?   yes/no

13. If you double the length of the sides of the square, will the perimeter double?   yes/no

Name _____ Date _____

EXERCISE 24: LEARNING MORE ABOUT CIRCLES (CONTINUED)

Let's Find Out!

14. Draw a circle with a diameter double the size of the diameter in the first circle.

15. The diameter of the circle drawn is (a)_____ (b) inches / square inches.

16. The radius of the circle drawn is (a)_____ (b) inches / square inches.

17. The area of the circle drawn is (a) _____ (b) inches / square inches.

18. The circumference of the circle drawn is (a) _____ (b) inches / square inches.

19. Draw a square over the circle you drew. Draw the square so the circle is completely inside the circle with the edge of the circle touching each of the four sides of the square but not overlapping outside the square.

20. Each side of the square is (a) _____ (b) inches / square inches.

21. The perimeter of the square is (a) _____ (b) inches / square inches.

22. The area of the square is (a) _____ (b) inches / square inches.

23. In the space below write what happens to the perimeter and area of a square as the length of the sides are doubled.

_____

_____

_____

Name _____ Date _____

EXERCISE 25: FINDING THE AREA OF COMBINED PLANE FIGURES

Calculate the area of each of the figures shown below. In the space provided below, explain the steps you took in order to work the problems.

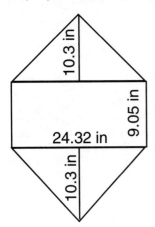

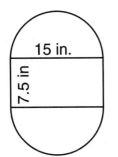

EXPLANATION

1. _____
   _____
   _____
   _____
   _____
   _____

   Answer: _____

2. _____
   _____
   _____
   _____
   _____

   Answer: _____

3. _____
   _____
   _____
   _____
   _____
   _____

   Answer: _____

4. _____
   _____
   _____
   _____
   _____
   _____

   Answer: _____

Name _____ Date _____

CHECKING YOUR UNDERSTANDING OF PLANE FIGURES

This exercise will check your understanding of plane figures and how to find the areas of these figures. It will also provide an opportunity to improve your organizational skills as well as your ability to communicate your knowledge to others.

EXERCISE 26

Your teacher feels that you understand plane figures so well that she has asked you to teach a group of younger students how to determine the areas of different plane figures. She says you should specifically explain how to figure the areas of squares, rectangles, triangles, parallelograms, and circles. In preparation for your class, complete the following. Don't worry! You won't really be teaching a class. You will just be deciding what material should be presented and how it should be organized.

List the points you intend to make in your presentation.

_____

_____

_____

_____

_____

_____

_____

Put these points in the order you plan to present them. Arrange these points in outline form in order to organize your thoughts. The main points should be Roman numerals (I, II, III, etc.). The subheadings that support these main points should be labeled with capital letters (A, B, C, etc.).

_____

_____

_____

_____

_____

_____

_____

Name _____ Date _____

EXERCISE 26 (CONTINUED)

List the most important points you will want the students to remember after you have finished with your presentation.

_____
_____
_____
_____

What could you do to emphasize these points?

_____
_____
_____
_____

List the areas you feel the students might have difficulty in understanding.

_____
_____
_____

What can you do to make these areas clearer?

_____
_____
_____
_____

Name _____ Date _____

EXERCISE 26 (CONTINUED)

Would graphics make your presentation better? Graphics are pictures, charts, slides, overhead transparencies or any other kind of visual you can create. What graphics would you use? Describe them.

_____

_____

_____

_____

_____

Write the introduction to your presentation.

_____

_____

_____

_____

_____

_____

_____

Write the conclusion to your presentation.

_____

_____

_____

_____

_____

_____

_____

Name _____ Date _____

Using Calculators on Tests
EXERCISE 27

For several years teachers, students, and parents have debated the question, "Should students be allowed to use calculators when they take mathematics tests?" This is your opportunity to state your opinion along with the logical reasons you used to support that opinion. In the space below, list all of the reasons, both for and against, the statement: *Students should be allowed to use calculators when they take mathematics tests.*

YES	**No**
1. _____	1. _____
2. _____	2. _____
3. _____	3. _____
4. _____	4. _____
5. _____	5. _____
6. _____	6. _____

While you may not be able to think of six reasons both for and against the topic, it is important that you list every possible reason you can think of. It is especially important for you to spend as much thought in listing the reasons that do not support your position as you do on those reasons that do support your position. You may find that your initial feeling concerning this topic changes when you see all of the good reasons on the other side. Also, if you know the reasons on the other side of the question, you are better able to offer a counterargument concerning these reasons.

Use the list you have just created to write a persuasive letter to the board of education encouraging them to adopt a school district policy either to let students use calculators on math tests or to forbid them from doing so. Your letter should be respectful, courteous, and logical.

Part One: The first part of your letter should state who you are, why you are writing, and your position on the question.

Part Two: The main part of your letter should include not only the reasons you feel as you do, but also a discussion of these reasons. You should also use your list above to anticipate arguments on the other side and include counterarguments for these reasons.

Conclusion: Your conclusion should summarize your position, encourage the board to support that position, and suggest some action you would like them to take.

Name _____ Date _____

Writing Word Problems
EXERCISE 28: PIZZA

In this exercise, you are to write word problems based on the following word: **Pizza**. Use your imagination, and create any facts or figures you choose. You may write about the restaurant, the food, the customers, or whatever you choose as long as it refers to pizza in some way. After you write the problem, show the solution and include the answer.

1. Write a word problem involving addition of fractions: _____

_____

_____

2. Write a word problem involving subtraction of fractions: _____

_____

_____

3. Write a word problem involving addition of decimals: _____

_____

_____

4. Write a word problem involving subtraction of decimals: _____

_____

_____

5. Write a word problem involving percentage: _____

_____

_____

6. Write a word problem involving ratio: _____

_____

_____

7. Write a word problem involving a pie graph: _____

_____

_____

Name _____ Date _____

Writing Word Problems
EXERCISE 29: SCHOOL

In this exercise, you are to write word problems based on the following word: **School**. Use your imagination to create any facts or figures you choose. You may write about the building, the cafeteria, the teachers, students, classes, or whatever you choose as long as it refers to school in some way. After you write the problem, show the solution and include the answer.

1. Write a word problem involving multiplication of fractions: _____

_____

_____

2. Write a word problem involving division of fractions: _____

_____

_____

3. Write a word problem involving multiplication of decimals: _____

_____

_____

4. Write a word problem involving division of decimals: _____

_____

_____

5. Write a word problem involving percentage: _____

_____

_____

6. Write a word problem involving ratio: _____

_____

_____

7. Write a word problem involving the creation of a table: _____

_____

_____

Name _____ Date _____

Writing Word Problems
EXERCISE 30: FOOTBALL

   Write word problems based on the following word: **Football**. Use your imagination, and create any facts or figures you choose. You may write about the stadium, the game, the fans, the players, the snacks, or whatever you choose, as long as it refers to football in some way. After you write the problem, show the solution and include the answer.

1. Write a word problem involving percentage: _____

_____

_____

2. Write a word problem involving ratio: _____

_____

_____

3. Write a word problem involving finding an average: _____

_____

_____

4. Write a word problem involving finding a range: _____

_____

_____

5. Write a word problem involving perimeter: _____

_____

_____

6. Write a word problem involving positive and negative numbers: _____

_____

_____

7. Write a word problem involving a line graph: _____

_____

_____

Name _____ Date _____

Writing Word Problems
EXERCISE 31: TEMPERATURE

Write word problems based on the following word: **Temperature**. Use your imagination to create any facts or figures you choose. You may write about the weather, climates, thermometers, or whatever you choose as long as it refers to temperature in some way. After you write the problem, show the solution and include the answer.

1. Write a word problem involving an equation: _____

_____

_____

_____

2. Write a word problem involving measurement: _____

_____

_____

_____

3. Write a word problem involving time: _____

_____

_____

_____

4. Write a word problem involving area or volume: _____

_____

_____

_____

5. Write a word problem involving a bar graph: _____

_____

_____

_____

Name _____ Date _____

Writing Math Essays
EXERCISE 32

Choose among the following topics and write an essay. The topics are broad and you may choose to narrow your composition to just a small part of the topic. Just below each essay topic is a list of items you might want to consider as you write your essay. These ideas are not in any order and should only be starting points for your research. You will not use all of these ideas, and you will think of other topics to include in your essay.

CALENDARS

- What is the importance of the calendar?
- On what is a calendar based?
- How did our current calendar consisting of 365 days a year, an extra day called leap year every four years, and 12 months with 28 to 31 days each month evolve?
- Trace the history of calendar making.
- What were the earliest calendars based on?
- What were some early calendars? How did they differ from one another?
- How did the months in our calendar get their names?
- How did the days in our calendar get their names?
- What are equinoxes, and how do they relate to calendars?
- What is a solstice, when does one occur, and how do they affect the calendar? What is it based on?
- What other calendars are currently used today?
- What are some suggestions for calendar improvement?

TIME

- Why is it important to have a universal method of recording time?
- Ancient methods for keeping time
- Time Zones
- Clocks, watches, and other devices
- Daylight Savings Time
- Light Year
- Standard Time
- International Date Line
- Greenwich, England
- Solar Time
- Atomic Clock
- Relativity

Name _____ Date _____

EXERCISE 32 (CONTINUED) WEIGHTS AND MEASURES

- Ancient methods for measuring and weighing
- Why is a uniform measurement system important?
- Metrics
- Conventional System
- National Bureau of Standards
- Avoirdupois
- British Thermal Unit
- Calorie
- Celsius
- Centigrade
- Compass
- Lumen
- Troy Weight
- Absolute Zero
- What are the advantages and disadvantages of the various measuring and weighing systems?

NUMBERS

- Numbering Systems
- Decimal System
- Binary System
- Numerals
- Arabic
- Roman
- Prime Numbers
- Rational Numbers
- Irrational Numbers
- Imaginary Numbers
- Complex Numbers
- Pythagoras
- Integers
- Exponent
- Zero
- Fraction
- Ancient Mathematical Characters

Name _____ Date _____

Writing and Thinking About Ratio

Adams Junior High School has 500 students and 20 teachers. Of the 20 teachers, two teach computer skills. How can you best compare the number of computer teachers with the total number of teachers? There are several ways, but one of the more useful ways is to compare them by division. When you compare two numbers by division, you are finding the ratio of these numbers. Ratios are fractions. They can be proper fractions such as $\frac{2}{20}$ or they may be improper fractions such as $\frac{20}{2}$.

It can easily be seen that the ratio $\frac{2}{20}$ can be reduced to $\frac{1}{10}$. This ratio can be expressed in one of the following ways:

- one to ten (In words)   • 1:10 (Colon notation)   • $\frac{1}{10}$ or 1/10 (Fraction notation)

What we are basically saying is that the ratio of computer teachers to the total number of teachers in Adams Junior High School is 1:10.

This same ratio may also be expressed comparing the total number of teachers in Adams Junior High School with the number of computer teachers. In other words it can be expressed as

- ten to one   • 10:1   • $\frac{10}{1}$ or 10/1

EXERCISE 33: CREATING EXAMPLES OF RATIO

Using the above example of Adams Junior High School, you are to create other ratios that might be found. You may use any aspect of the school for your examples. Be creative. You can include teachers, classes, students, clubs, the cafeteria, or any other topic you might imagine. The first is given as an example.

ITEM	RATIO
1. Two computer teachers out of 20 teachers	1:10
2.	
3.	
4.	
5.	
6.	
7.	
8.	
9.	
10.	
11.	
12.	
13.	
14.	
15.	

Name_____ Date_____

Writing to Understand Our Number System

The number system used in the United States is a decimal system based on ten. It is a number system that was invented in India and taken to the Arab world, therefore, it is known as the **Hindu-Arabic decimal system**. The numerals used in the system are 0, 1, 2, 3, 4, 5, 6, 7, 8, 9. The number system developed gradually over a long period of time to become the system we use today.

There are several different kinds of numbers within the Hindu-Arabic decimal system. Examples are listed below.

The **natural numbers** are : 1, 2, 3, 4, 5, 6 . . .
The **whole numbers** are: 0, 1, 2, 3, 4, 5, 6 . . .
The **integer numbers** are : . . . -6, -5, -4, -3, -2, -1, 0, +1, +2, +3, +4, +5, +6 . . .
The **rational numbers** include the integers and fractions that are repeating or terminating decimals.

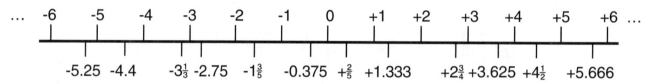

All **rational numbers** can be located at a specific point on the number line. For example, the integers - 6 and + 6 can be located exactly. The fractions - $\frac{7}{8}$ and + $\frac{2}{3}$ can be located exactly. You will find, however, that not every fraction can be located at a specific point on the number line. Those numbers that cannot be located at a specific point on the number line are not part of the rational numbers.

All rational numbers may be written as decimals that are either terminating or repeating decimals. A **terminating decimal** is one that ends in zero. A **repeating decimal** is one that has a decimal pattern that keeps repeating.

Example: Terminating decimal. $\frac{7}{8}$ = 0.875 If carried out farther, a string of repeating zeros would result. 0.87500000 Seven-eights is an example of a terminating decimal.
Convert the fraction $\frac{3}{8}$ to its decimal equivalent. $\frac{3}{8}$ = 0.375, which is a terminating decimal. It can be located at a specific point on the number line.

Example: Repeating decimal. $\frac{2}{3}$ = 0.666666666… If carried out farther, an infinite string of 6's will always result. Two-thirds is an example of a decimal with a repeating pattern, but two-thirds can be located at a specific point on the number line.
Convert the fraction $\frac{1}{3}$ to its decimal equivalent. $\frac{1}{3}$ = 0.3333333333, which is a repeating decimal. It can be located at a specific point on the number line.

The **irrational numbers** are numbers that cannot be located at a specific point on the number line. Irrational numbers written in decimal form are nonrepeating.

Example: Nonrepeating decimal. $\sqrt{7}$ = 2.645751311…. If carried out farther, a string of nonrepeating numbers will continue. There is no specific point for the decimal on the number line. There are many irrational numbers.

46

Name _____ Date _____

EXERCISE 34: DETERMINING IF A NUMBER IS RATIONAL OR IRRATIONAL

The irrational numbers include all of the fractions and decimals that cannot be located at a specific point on the number line.

In the next exercise a calculator will be needed. Determine if the fractions below are rational or irrational numbers. For each of the problems, write the decimal equivalent and indicate by using an X if the number is a terminating, repeating, or nonrepeating decimal and if the number is rational or irrational.

	Decimal Form	Repeating	Nonrepeating	Terminating	Rational	Irrational
1. $\frac{7}{8}$ =	_____	____	____	____	____	____
2. $\frac{2}{3}$ =	_____	____	____	____	____	____
3. $\frac{2}{7}$ =	_____	____	____	____	____	____
4. $\frac{5}{6}$ =	_____	____	____	____	____	____
5. $\frac{5}{7}$ =	_____	____	____	____	____	____
6. $\frac{8}{9}$ =	_____	____	____	____	____	____
7. $\frac{2}{4}$ =	_____	____	____	____	____	____
8. $\frac{11}{14}$ =	_____	____	____	____	____	____
9. $\frac{16}{17}$ =	_____	____	____	____	____	____
10. $\frac{21}{22}$ =	_____	____	____	____	____	____
11. $\sqrt{2}$ =	_____	____	____	____	____	____
12. $\sqrt{5}$ =	_____	____	____	____	____	____
13. $\sqrt{17}$ =	_____	____	____	____	____	____
14. $\sqrt{4}$ =	_____	____	____	____	____	____
15. $\sqrt{64}$ =	_____	____	____	____	____	____
16. $\sqrt{256}$ =	_____	____	____	____	____	____
17. $\sqrt{31}$ =	_____	____	____	____	____	____
18. $\sqrt{81}$ =	_____	____	____	____	____	____
19. $\sqrt{121}$ =	_____	____	____	____	____	____
20. $\sqrt{60}$ =	_____	____	____	____	____	____

Name _____ Date _____

EXERCISE 35: WHAT WOULD YOU DO?

1. You are working in a department store in the men's section. An individual comes in and wants to purchase a sweater that costs $45.

    The individual has only $38. You show him that $7 is needed by subtracting $45 from $38 and getting $-7. The individual is confused because he does not understand any number system other than the whole numbers. In the space below tell how you might make the individual understand how many additional dollars are needed to purchase the sweater.

_____

_____

_____

    Below you will find statements that might be made by individuals at sporting events. On the space below each statement rewrite the statement as it might be made if the only number systems were the natural and whole numbers. You cannot use negative numbers, fractions, percents, or decimals, so any part of the statement using negative numbers, decimals, percents, or fractions must be changed.

    Use quotation marks and the proper punctuation in your rewriting.

2. The announcer said, "The game is now in the top half of the seventh inning."

_____

_____

3. The game analyst said, "Johnson, the fullback for the Blazers, is now minus 12 yards."

_____

_____

4. The play-by-play announcer stated, "The Bullets must improve their free-throw shooting. They are now making 68 percent of their free throws."

_____

_____

_____

_____

Name _____ Date _____

EXERCISE 35: WHAT WOULD YOU DO? (CONTINUED)

5. "He is now hitting .200 for the season," drawled the announcer. "He needs to be hitting at least .250."

_____

_____

6. "Men," the coach shouted, "We need to run two-thirds of the time and pass one-third."

_____

_____

7. The manager said, "We are out of size $12\frac{1}{2}$ high-top shoes. We have a number of pairs of size $11\frac{1}{2}$."

_____

_____

8. The band director said, "We have got to do a better job of playing the quarter notes."

_____

_____

9. The ticket seller said, "That will be $7.50 for the two adults. The child will have to pay $1.75."

_____

_____

10. On the blanks below write some other things in our lives that would need to change if the rational number system were not available for use. (Think about clothes, cars, groceries, and so on.)

_____

_____

_____

_____

_____

_____

_____

_____

Name _____ Date _____

EXERCISE 36: ORGANIZING PARAGRAPHS

A very important skill in understanding mathematics is learning to organize our thoughts. Developing good writing skills can help develop organizational skills that can be useful in mathematics.

In the following writing exercise you will be learning to develop paragraphs. Each paragraph should have the following three main parts.

Topic Sentence: Tells what you want to write about.
Middle Sentences: Explain and add details about the topic sentence.
Closing Sentence: A sentence that restates the topic sentence in a different way and adds more information.

In this exercise you are to write a paragraph with a topic sentence, middle sentences, and a closing sentence. Use the sentences below to form the paragraph. The topic sentence and closing sentences are in bold. Place the numbers from 1 to 7 on the blanks beside the sentences to indicate the order in which they should be written in the paragraph. The number 1 will be the topic sentence. The number 7 will be the closing sentence. The numbers 2, 3, 4, 5, and 6 are to be used for the middle sentences.

_____ It has a repeating decimal and can be located at a specific point on the number line.
_____ The square root of seven is an irrational number.
_____ **The real number system includes the rational and irrational numbers.**
_____ It has a nonrepeating decimal and cannot be located at a specific point on the number line.
_____ **The real number system is very important, because the rational and irrational numbers make it possible to solve many more mathematics problems.**
_____ Two-thirds is a rational number.
_____ Irrational numbers are numbers that have nonrepeating decimals. Rational numbers are numbers that have terminating or repeating decimals.

On the blanks that follow, write a paragraph using the seven sentences above.

Real Numbers

Topic sentence: _____

_____

Middle sentences: _____

_____

_____

_____

_____

Closing sentence: _____

_____

Name_____ Date _____

EXERCISE 36: ORGANIZING PARAGRAPHS (CONTINUED)

Now write a paragraph about the whole number system. Make sure that you include a topic sentence, middle sentences, and a closing sentence.

Whole Numbers

Topic Sentence:_____

_____

Middle Sentences: _____

_____

_____

_____

_____

Closing Sentence: _____

_____

In much of your writing, it will be necessary to write using more than one paragraph. In the next exercise you will write longer selections of more than one paragraph.

Name _____ Date _____

EXERCISE 37: DESCRIPTIVE WRITING

It is often necessary to describe a topic in writing. This type of writing is called *descriptive writing.* In preparing for the next exercise, imagine that you are going to write and describe the integer number system to another person. You are going to use three paragraphs to complete the description. The three paragraphs are to be written using the following guidelines.

First Paragraph: Tells what the integer numbers are.
Second Paragraph: Explains or illustrates the integer number system.
Third Paragraph: Summarizes the integer number system.

When preparing to write about a topic, it is important to first review all of the information you have on the topic. In preparing for the descriptive writing exercise, complete the following to review the integer numbers.

1. The integer numbers are _____ . . .

2. The integer numbers are different from the whole numbers because _____

_____

_____

3. The integer numbers are different from the rational numbers because _____

_____

_____

4. The integers may be used to _____

_____

5. The integer numbers cannot be used to _____

_____

6. The integer numbers were an important step in the development of our number system because

_____

_____

_____

Name _____ Date _____

EXERCISE 37: DESCRIPTIVE WRITING (CONTINUED)

7. On the blanks below write a description of the integer number system. Remember to include three paragraphs, following the guidelines on the previous page.

The Integer Numbers

First Paragraph: Describe or tell something about the integer numbers.

_____

_____

_____

_____

Second Paragraph: Explain or illustrate the integer numbers. Tell what you know about the integer numbers such as characteristics, how they are used, and so on.

_____

_____

_____

_____

_____

_____

_____

Third Paragraph: Give a summary statement about the integer numbers. Tell the reader why integers are important.

_____

_____

_____

_____

Name_____ Date _____

EXERCISE 38: UNDERSTANDING AND USING MATHEMATIC SYMBOLS

Mathematics uses symbols to communicate, much like words are used to communicate in reading and writing. The following are some of the symbols that are used in mathematics. Once you understand the symbols, it is much easier to understand math problems.

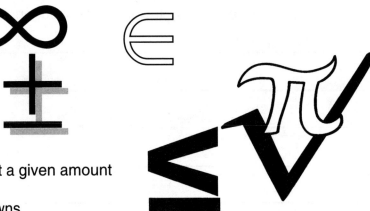

-	Minus; subtract or find the difference
+	Plus; add or find the sum
x, *, •	Multiply or find the product
=	Equals
≤	Is equal to or less than
≥	Is equal to or greater than
÷ or /	Divide or find the quotient
√	Radical sign for finding the square root of
≠	Does not equal
π	Means 3.14 or pi and is used when finding the circumference or area of a circle
≃	Is congruent to
≈	Is similar to
∉	Is not an element of
∈	Is an element of
Ø	Is an empty set
{. . .}	A set
⊆	A subset
1—1	Correspondence
%	Percent sign
∞	Goes on to infinity
±	Plus or minus; add or subtract a given amount
°	The degree sign
x or y	Letters used to signify unknowns

In the following sentences, mathematical symbols have been used in place of words. Rewrite the sentences using words for the mathematical symbols. Not all of the above symbols will be used. Do not change the meaning of the sentences.

1. I went to the party − some of my best friends.

_____

2. After meeting some new people, I found that my best friends' absence ≠ having a poor time.

_____

_____

3. In the future I will ÷ my time amongst my old and new friends.

_____

Name_____ Date _____

EXERCISE 38: UNDERSTANDING AND USING MATHEMATIC SYMBOLS (CONT.)

4. The different individuals attending the party were ≈ so everyone had a great time.

_____

5. Since I was from a different school, I was able to + a great deal to the conversations.

_____

6. The refreshments for the evening were great. The chocolate π was ≥ the oatmeal cookies.

_____

_____

7. There was not one $\sqrt{}$ individual attending the party.

_____

8. All of the people attending the party made up a { . . . }.

_____

9. The girls were a ⊆ of the { . . .} of people at the party.

_____

10. There was the same number of boys and girls, a 1—1 correspondence.

_____

11. There were 50 people at the party ± four.

_____

Fill in the blanks.

12. The number at the party was between ____ and ____ .

13. Since there was a 1—1 correspondence between boys and girls, the percentage of boys was _____ percent. That means there was/were _____ boy(s) for every girl at the party.

   In mathematics, symbols are a shorthand method of expressing information. In the following section a mathematical statement or formula will be given. Write a statement that tells what the mathematical statement or formula says and a statement to explain how the answer for each is determined.

14. $x^2 = 16$ _____

15. $x^4 = 64$ _____

16. $x = \sqrt{16}$ _____

17. $y = \sqrt{64}$ _____

Name _____ Date _____

EXERCISE 39: MATHEMATIC SYMBOLS CROSSWORD PUZZLE

Use the clues below and the information about mathematic symbols that you have learned to complete the puzzle.

ACROSS

2. This (°) is a _____ sign.
3. This sign (≃) means _____.
7. This sign (*) means _____ .
10. This sign (+) is a _____ sign.
14. This sign (±) means _____ __ _____ .
16. This sign (÷) means _____ .
17. In the algebraic symbol (x^2), the number 2 is an____.
18. This sign (-) is a _____ sign.
19. This sign (∞) means _____ .

DOWN

1. Is the opposite of subtraction
4. This sign (≠) means _____ _____ .
5. This sign (=) means _____ .
6. This sign (≥) means _____ than or equal to.
8. This sign (≤) means _____ than or equal to.
9. This sign (√) is a _____ sign.
11. Is the opposite of multiplication
12. This sign (%) means _____ .
13. $\frac{2}{5}$ is a _____ .
14. This sign (π) means _____ .
15. This (x) is an _____ quantity.

Name _____ Date _____

EXERCISE 40: WRITING ABOUT MATHEMATIC FORMULAS

Listed below are formulas that are used in the study of mathematics. Write a paragraph describing each of the following formulas. Write as though the person who will be reading the paragraph doesn't understand anything about the letters, symbols, or numbers in the formulas. In the opening sentence of the paragraph, tell what the formula means. In sentences that follow describe each of the letters, numbers, or symbols so that the reader will have a visual picture of what each letter, number, or symbol really means. Your last sentence should restate what the formula is designed to find.

Circle   C (Circumference) π (Pi or 3.14)   d(diameter)
1. $C = \pi d$

_____
_____
_____
_____
_____
_____

Circle   A (area) π (pi or 3.14)   r(radius)
2. $A = \pi r^2$

_____
_____
_____
_____
_____

Square   P (perimeter)   s (side)
3. $P = 4s$

_____
_____
_____
_____
_____

Name _____ Date _____

EXERCISE 40: WRITING ABOUT MATHEMATIC FORMULAS (CONTINUED)

Square   A (area)   s (side)

4. $A = s^2$

_____

_____

_____

_____

_____

Sphere   V (volume)   4/3 (4 divided by 3) π (pi or 3.14)   r (radius)

5. $V = 4/3\ \pi r^3$

_____

_____

_____

_____

_____

Cube   V (volume)   s (side)

6. $V = s^3$

_____

_____

_____

_____

_____

Name _____   Date _____

Square Root
EXERCISE 41: FINDING SQUARE ROOTS

The symbol for finding the square root is the radical sign $\sqrt{}$. To find the square root of a number is to find the number that, multiplied times itself, results in the number under the radical.

Example: Find $\sqrt{25}$. What number times itself will yield 25?
$5 \times 5 = 25$ so the square root of 25 is 5.

Find the square root of each of the following.

1. $\sqrt{9}$ = _____

2. $\sqrt{16}$ = _____

3. $\sqrt{36}$ = _____

4. $\sqrt{81}$ = _____

5. $\sqrt{144}$ = _____

6. $\sqrt{121}$ = _____

7. $\sqrt{1}$ = _____

8. $\sqrt{4}$ = _____

9. $\sqrt{100}$ = _____

10. $\sqrt{49}$ = _____

11. $\sqrt{25}$ = _____

12. $\sqrt{64}$ = _____

13. $\sqrt{324}$ = _____

14. $\sqrt{625}$ = _____

15. $\sqrt{400}$ = _____

Name _____ Date _____

EXERCISE 42: SQUARE ROOT SENTENCES

Each of the odd-numbered statements (1, 3, 5, 7, 9) in the exercise below has two simple sentences. Rewrite the simple sentences as compound sentences connected by one of the conjunctions "and," "or," "but," "for," or "yet."

Using the numbers from Exercise 41, complete the blanks in each of the even-numbered statements (2, 4, 6, 8, 10), which explain what numbers are referred to in the odd-numbered statements.

1. My square root is one more than yours. I'm 19 greater than you.

_____

_____

2. I am the number a) _____ , so you must be b) _____ .

3. My square root is twice yours. I am four times greater than you.

_____

_____

4. I am the number a) _____ , and you are the number b) _____ .

5. I am one-fourth of you. My square root is one-half of yours.

_____

_____

6. I am the number a) _____ , and you are the number b) _____ .

7. We are both even numbers. I am 28 greater than you.

_____

_____

8. You are the number a) _____ , and I am the number b) _____ .

9. We are both odd numbers. Your square root is 3 times greater than mine.

_____

_____

10. You are the number a) _____ , and I am the number b) _____ .

Name_____ Date _____

EXERCISE 43: DIALOGUE AMONG NUMBERS

Dialogue is the conversation (communication) between two or more speakers. In this exercise you will learn to write using dialogue. In writing dialogue, use the following guidelines.

1. Pairs of quotation marks (" ") are used to enclose the actual words of each speaker.
2. Periods and commas go inside the quotation marks.
3. A new paragraph is begun for each new speaker.

speaker   actual words of speaker   period inside quotations
Example: John said, "Number patterns are interesting."

Use the numbers and square roots below to develop dialogue that might occur between the numbers. Remember: the numbers will be the speakers. Statements about the square roots will be the words of the speakers (numbers). Be creative, but base the dialogue on patterns and facts about the sets of numbers.

Numbers: 1, 4, 9, 16, 25, 36, 49, 64, 81, 100, 121, 144
Square Roots: 1, 2, 3,   4,   5,   6,   7,   8,   9,   10,   11,   12

1. Write the dialogue that might occur among the numbers 1, 9, 25, 49, 81, and 121. Let's look at some of the characteristics of these numbers that might help start the dialogue:
   They are all odd numbers.
   The increase from number to number is an even number.
   Do you notice anything about their square roots?
   Think about what one number might say to another.
   What might 9 say to 81? or 81 to 9?
   What might odd numbers say about even numbers?

_____

_____

_____

_____

_____

_____

_____

_____

_____

_____

Name _____ Date _____

EXERCISE 43: DIALOGUE AMONG NUMBERS (CONTINUED)

2. Write the dialogue that might occur between the numbers 2, 4, 16, 36, 64, 100, and 144. Let's look at some of the characteristics of these numbers that might help start the dialogue.

     They are all even numbers.
     What about the change in size from one number to the next?
     What about their square roots?
     Think about what one number might say to another.
     What might 64 say to 16? 16 to 64?
     What might even numbers say about odd numbers?

_____

_____

_____

_____

_____

_____

_____

_____

_____

_____

_____

_____

_____

_____

_____

_____

_____

_____

_____

Name _____ Date _____

Learning About Exponents
EXERCISE 44: EXPONENT PROBLEMS AND DIALOGUE

Exponents tell the power to which a number is to be raised.

Examples:

2^2 is read "two to the second power." The exponent tells you to multiply two times two. $2 \times 2 = 4$ So $2^2 = 4$

3^3 is read "three to the third power." The exponent tells you to multiply three times three times three. $3 \times 3 \times 3 = 27$ So $3^3 = 27$

Complete the following by performing the multiplication indicated by the exponents:

1. $1^2 =$ _____   2. $2^2 =$ _____   3. $3^2 =$ _____   4. $4^2 =$ _____

5. $5^2 =$ _____   6. $6^2 =$ _____   7. $7^2 =$ _____

8. $1^3 =$ _____   9. $2^3 =$ _____   10. $3^3 =$ _____   11. $4^3 =$ _____

12. $5^3 =$ _____   13. $6^3 =$ _____   14. $7^3 =$ _____

15. $1^4 =$ _____   16. $2^4 =$ _____   17. $3^4 =$ _____   18. $4^4 =$ _____

19. $5^4 =$ _____   20. $6^4 =$ _____   21. $7^4 =$ _____

22. Refer to the above problems and write the dialogue that might occur among the numbers 1 through 7 as exponents are assigned to each number. Look for patterns. Patterns are important in mathematics. Be creative in your dialogue. Here are some examples that might help start the dialogue.

Number one said, "No matter how big my exponent, I'm the same old number."
Number two said, "Increase my exponent by one, and I'm twice as big."

_____

_____

_____

_____

_____

_____

_____

Name _____ Date _____

Learning About Other Number Systems

There have been many number systems in addition to the Base Ten system. One such number system is known as **Base Two**. Another system is known as **Base Five**.

EXERCISE 45: LEARNING ABOUT BASE TWO

The Base Two number system uses the two symbols 0 and 1. It is often called the **binary system**. This system has become very important in the development of computers.

The following are examples of Base Two numbers and Base Ten numbers.

Base Ten:	1	2	3	4	5	6	7	8	9	10
Base Two:	1	10	11	100	101	110	111	1000	1001	1010

Example 1: Expressing the Base Two number 111111 in Base Ten

$$\begin{array}{cccccc} 32\text{'s} & 16\text{'s} & 8\text{'s} & 4\text{'s} & 2\text{'s} & 1\text{'s} \end{array}$$
111111 Base Two =   1   1   1   1   1   1   = 63 Base Ten

Changing 111111 Base Two to 63 Base Ten
$$\begin{array}{cccccc} 32\text{'s} & 16\text{'s} & 8\text{'s} & 4\text{'s} & 2\text{'s} & 1\text{'s} \end{array}$$
1(32) + 1(16) + 1(8) + 1(4) + 1(2) + 1   = 63 Base Ten

Example 2: Expressing the Base Two number 1011 in Base Ten
1011 Base Two = 1(8) + 0(4) + 1(2) + 1(1) = 11 Base Ten

Refer to the examples and complete the following:

1. 1 Base Two = ——————— Base Ten

2. 10 Base Two = ——————— Base Ten

3. 100 Base Two = ——————— Base Ten

4. 1000 Base Two = ——————— Base Ten

5. 10000 Base Two = ——————— Base Ten

6. 100000 Base Two = ——————— Base Ten

7. 11 Base Two = ——————— Base Ten

8. 101 Base Two = ——————— Base Ten

9. 110 Base Two = ——————— Base Ten

10. 1011 Base Two = ——————— Base Ten

Name _____ Date _____

EXERCISE 45: LEARNING ABOUT BASE TWO (CONTINUED)

Write each of the following numbers as two with the correct exponent.

11. 4 = _____   12. 8 = _____   13. 16 = _____   14. 32 = _____

15. 64 = _____   16. 128 = _____

17. On the blanks above each number write the number two with the correct exponent.

$$\underset{\text{111111 Base Two} =}{} \quad \overset{a)\_\_\_}{1(32)} + \overset{b)\_\_\_}{1(16)} + \overset{c)\_\_}{1(8)} + \overset{d)\_\_}{1(4)} + \overset{2^1}{1(2)} + \overset{2^0}{1} = 63 \text{ Base Ten}$$

18. Fill in the blanks below with the number two and the correct exponent for Base Two.

$$\underset{\text{11111111 Base Two} =}{} \overset{a)\_\_}{1(128)} + \overset{b)\_\_}{1(64)} + \overset{2^5}{1(32)} + \overset{2^4}{1(16)} + \overset{2^3}{1(8)} + \overset{2^2}{1(4)} + \overset{2^1}{1(2)} + \overset{2^0}{1(1)} = c)\_\_ \text{ Base Ten}$$

Express the following Base Two numbers as Base Ten numbers.

19. 100010 Base Two = _____ Base Ten

20. 101000 Base Two = _____ Base Ten

21. 10001 Base Two = _____ Base Ten

22. 1001011 Base Two = _____ Base Ten

23. 111101 Base Two = _____ Base Ten

24. 11101 Base Two = _____ Base Ten

25. 10000010 Base Two = _____ Base Ten

Express the following Base Ten numbers as Base Two numbers.

26. 15 Base Ten = _____ Base Two

27. 35 Base Ten = _____ Base Two

28. 26 Base Ten = _____ Base Two

29. 20 Base Ten = _____ Base Two

30. 50 Base Ten = _____ Base Two

Name _____ Date _____

EXERCISE 46: LEARNING ABOUT BASE FIVE

The Base Five number system uses the five symbols 0, 1, 2, 3, 4.

The following are examples of how Base Five numbers are counted off compared to Base Ten numbers.

Base Ten:	1	2	3	4	5	6
Base Five:	1	2	3	4	10	11

Base Ten:	7	8	9	10	11	12
Base Five:	12	13	14	20	21	22

Reading numbers in bases other than Base Ten. The examples below using Base Five show how to read numbers expressed in bases other than Base Ten.

1321 Base Five is read "one, three, two, one" not "one thousand three hundred twenty-one."
2103 Base Five is read "two, one, zero, three" not "two thousand one hundred three."

On the blank next to each Base Five number write the way you should read the number.

1. 1433 Base Five " _____ "

2. 29 Base Five " _____ "

3. 221 Base Five " _____ "

4. 13211 Base Five " _____ "

5. 24313 Base Five " _____ "

Let's look at the following examples to determine how to express a Base Five number as a Base Ten number.

Example: Expressing the Base Five number 1321 in Base Ten.

$$1321 \text{ Base Five} = 1(5^3) + 3(5^2) + 2(5^1) + 1(5^0) = 211 \text{ Base Ten}$$

or:

$$\begin{array}{cccc} 5^3 & 5^2 & 5^1 & 5^0 \end{array}$$
$$1(125) + 3(25) + 2(5) + 1(1) = 211 \text{ Base Ten}$$

Example: Expressing the Base Five number 3411 in Base Ten.

$$3411 \text{ Base Five} = 3(5^3) + 4(5^2) + 1(5^1) + 1(5^0) = 481 \text{ Base Ten}$$

or:

$$\begin{array}{cccc} 5^3 & 5^2 & 5^1 & 5^0 \end{array}$$
$$3(125) + 4(25) + 1(5) + 1(1) = 481 \text{ Base Ten}$$

Name _____   Date _____

EXERCISE 46: LEARNING ABOUT BASE FIVE (CONTINUED)

Refer to the examples on the previous page and complete the following.

6. 1 Base Five = _____ Base Ten

7. 10 Base Five = _____ Base Ten

8. 100 Base Five = _____ Base Ten

9. 1000 Base Five = _____ Base Ten

10. 10000 Base Five = _____ Base Ten

11. 124 Base Five = _____ Base Ten

12. 2441 Base Five = _____ Base Ten

13. 111 Base Five = _____ Base Ten

14. 410 Base Five = _____ Base Ten

15. 233 Base Five = _____ Base Ten

Write the following numbers as five with the correct exponent.

16. 25 = _____   17. 125 = _____   18. 625 = _____   19. 3125 = _____

20. Write the numeral five with the correct exponent on the blank above each number.

$$\text{a)} \underline{\quad} \qquad \text{b)} \underline{\quad} \qquad \text{c)} \underline{\quad} \qquad \text{d)} \underline{\quad}$$
$$5 \qquad\qquad 5 \qquad\qquad 5 \qquad\qquad 5 \qquad 5^0$$

23241 Base Five = 2(625) + 3(125) + 2(25) + 4(5) + 1(1)   = 1696 Base Ten

Express the following Base Ten numbers as Base Five numbers.

21. 95 Base Ten = _____ Base Five

22. 1250 Base Ten = _____ Base Five

23. 862 Base Ten = _____ Base Five

24. 1079 Base Ten = _____ Base Five

25. 43 Base Ten = _____ Base Five

Name _____ Date _____

EXERCISE 47: WRITING EXERCISE FOR NUMBER BASES

Situation: You have visited a cousin during the summer. Now you are back in school. In mathematics class you have been studying Base Ten, Base Five, and Base Two. In writing class you have been learning about writing friendly letters that describe.

Directions: On your own paper write a friendly letter to your cousin describing either Base Two or Base Five. Your goal is to write the description so your cousin will understand Base Two or Base Five. In your description think of adjectives and adverbs that will make your writing more alive. Tell why you like or dislike the number system. You might tell how it is like or unlike Base Ten. Make sure your letter has an inside address, greeting, and salutation. Write using complete sentences. Check your letter for grammar and punctuation. Write legibly and keep your letter neat.

Your teacher will use the following to grade your letter. You should use these guidelines to check your letter before handing it in for grading.

Grade   **Guidelines**

4   Writing is legible. Letter is neat. Letter has inside address, greeting, and salutation. Sentences are complete, with subject and predicate. The number system has been described. The descriptions include examples so that the reader has a clear understanding of the number system. Adjectives and adverbs are used in the sentences to make the reading more interesting. Opening sentence clearly tells the reader what the letter is about. Sentences show variety of simple, compound, and complex sentences. The body of the letter is organized so reader can understand the number system. Closing sentences include summary of writer's thoughts about the number system.

3   Writing is legible. Letter is neat. Letter has inside address, greeting, and salutation. Sentences are complete with subject and predicate. The number system has been described. The descriptions include examples so that the reader has a clear understanding of the number system. Adjectives and adverbs are used in the sentences to make the reading more interesting. Opening sentence clearly tells the reader what the letter is about. The body of the letter is organized so reader can understand the number system. Closing sentences are related to body of letter.

2   Writing is legible. Letter is neat. Letter has inside address, greeting, and salutation. Sentences are complete with subject and predicate. The number system has been described. Opening sentence tells what the letter is about, body of the letter describes the number system, closing sentences are related to the body of the letter.

1   Writing is legible. Letter is neat. Letter has inside address, greeting, and salutation. Letter includes sentences about the number system.

0   Letter is not neatly written. Letter is not legible.

Name _____ Date _____

Learning About Prime and Composite Numbers

In learning about prime and composite numbers it is important to understand **factors**. Factors are two or more quantities that when multiplied together result in a product. **Prime numbers** have only two factors, the prime number and the number 1.

Example: The prime number 3 has two factors. The factors are 1 and 3. The number 3 is a prime number.

Composite numbers have additional factors other than the number one and the composite number.

Example: The number 6 has four factors. The factors are 1, 2, 3, and 6. $1 \times 6 = 6$ $2 \times 3 = 6$ Six is not a prime number, since it has the factors 2 and 3 in addition to 1 and 6.

The next example will show two ways to find the prime factors in a composite number. One way to find the prime factors in a composite number is to use a **factor tree**. Another way is to set up a **division problem**. Both ways require you to perform division.

Example: Composite number 6. Divide 6 by 2. The prime factors are 2 and 3.

<table>
<tr><td align="center">**Factor Tree**</td><td align="center">**Division Model**</td></tr>
<tr><td align="center">6
╱ ╲
② ③</td><td align="center">3
2)6
6
―
0</td></tr>
<tr><td align="center">Prime factors are 2 and 3</td><td align="center">Prime factors are 2 and 3</td></tr>
</table>

Example: Composite number 12. Divide 12 by 2. The factors are 2 and 6. Now divide 6 by 2. The factors are 2 and 3. (Note the division problem is designed upside down so that the factors are easier to determine.) The prime factors of 12 are 2, 2, and 3. The 2, 2 can be written as 2^2. So the prime factors are 2^2, 3.

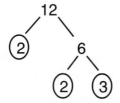

Example: Composite number 81. Eighty-one is not divisible by 2 so try 3. Divide 81 by 3. The factors are 3 and 27. Now 27 is not divisible by 2 so try 3. Divide 27 by 3, and the factors are 3 and 9. Next divide 9 by 3, and the factor is 3. So the prime factors of 81 are 3, 3, 3, 3 or 3^4.

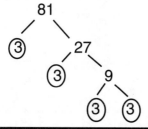

Name _____   Date _____

EXERCISE 48: FINDING FACTORS

Find the prime factors for each of the following using either the factor tree or the division method. Show your work.

1. 8 = _____   2. 15 = _____   3. 25 = _____   4. 100 = _____

5. 16 = _____   6. 19 = _____   7. 44 = _____   8. 11 = _____

9. 7 = _____   10. 9 = _____   11. 31 = _____   12. 32 = _____

13. 21 = _____   14. 50 = _____   15. 26 = _____   16. 78 = _____

17. 90 = _____   18. 81 = _____   19. 57 = _____   20. 98 = _____

Name_____ Date _____

Learning to Use Comparison and Contrast in Writing

Using the compare and contrast method of writing can be very effective in explaining a topic. When **comparing**, the writer tells how one thing is like another, and when **contrasting**, the writer tells how one thing is unlike another. When preparing to write using the compare or contrast method, it is important to organize the topic(s) you are going to write about so that you can determine what is alike and/or unlike about the topic(s).

EXERCISE 49: WRITING TO CONTRAST

Read each statement below about prime and composite numbers, and place the number for the statement under one of the two categories.

Statements

1. They are all odd numbers, except for the number two.

2. The only factors are the number and the number one.

3. These numbers have factors besides the number and the number one.

4. The factors of these numbers are often expressed with an exponent.

5. When two of these are added, the result is an even number.

6. These numbers are never prime.

7. Twenty-six, forty-four, and four are examples.

8. Seventeen, three, and thirty-seven are examples.

9. The odd numbers nine, thirty-nine, and fifty-one are examples.

10. The odd numbers seven, eleven, and forty-seven are examples.

11. Cannot be written as the product of two factors smaller than itself.

12. Can be written as the product of two factors smaller than itself.

Prime Number Statement   **Composite Number Statement**

_____ _____   _____ _____

_____ _____   _____ _____

_____ _____   _____ _____

_____ _____   _____ _____

_____ _____   _____ _____

Name _____ Date _____

EXERCISE 49: WRITING TO CONTRAST (CONTINUED)

13. You will use the information from the statements on the previous page to contrast the prime and composite numbers. You are going to tell how they are different. You will need a topic sentence that introduces the paragraph. You may use one of your own or select a topic sentence from one of the following.

The natural numbers can be divided into the prime and composite numbers.
The prime and composite numbers are natural numbers.
The natural number system includes two very important sets of numbers.

Topic sentence:

_____

_____

Tell how the numbers are different:

_____

_____

_____

_____

_____

_____

_____

_____

_____

_____

Ending sentence:

_____

_____

Name _____ Date _____

EXERCISE 50: SIGNAL WORDS USED TO CONTRAST

A good time to learn about signal words is when studying contrast writing. **Signal words** are words that can be used to alert the reader that a change in thought will be presented. Signal words or phrases that indicate a change in thought will be presented are **however**, **nevertheless**, **on the other hand**, **instead**, **in contrast**, **but**, **yet**, and **still**.

Example sentences without signal words:
The odd numbers are numbers like three, five, and seven. All odd numbers are not prime. (Simple sentences without a signal word to the reader)

Example sentence with signal word:
The odd numbers are numbers like three, five and seven; however, all odd numbers are not prime. (Note that *however* signals the reader that a different thought is presented.)

The following exercise includes sentences that are written without signal words. On the blanks below each group of sentences rewrite the two sentences into one sentence using one of the signal words indicated in parentheses.

1. The whole numbers are all positive. The integer numbers include positive and negative numbers. (but, however)

_____

_____

2. The irrational number $\sqrt{7}$ has a decimal that is nonrepeating. The rational number $\frac{3}{5}$ has a decimal that is terminating. (on the other hand, in contrast)

_____

_____

3. The prime numbers do not have factors smaller than the prime number itself. Composite numbers have factors that are smaller than the composite number . (in contrast, on the other hand, nevertheless)

_____

_____

4. The prime and composite numbers are natural numbers. There is a difference between the prime and composite numbers. (yet, still, however)

_____

_____

5. Prime numbers are odd numbers. All odd numbers are not prime numbers. (yet, nevertheless, still)

_____

_____

Name _____ Date _____

EXERCISE 50: SIGNAL WORDS USED TO CONTRAST (CONTINUED)

In this exercise, you are to rewrite the contrast paragraph you wrote in Exercise 49 about prime and composite numbers. Rewrite the paragraph and combine sentences using the signal words. You may want to change some of your original sentences to use a signal word; however, it is not necessary that every sentence have a signal word.

_____

_____

_____

_____

_____

_____

_____

_____

_____

_____

_____

_____

_____

_____

_____

Name _____ Date _____

EXERCISE 51: WRITING TO COMPARE

In the exercise below are statements about rational and irrational numbers. Read each statement and place the number for the statement under one of the two categories. Some statements may refer to both categories.

Statements

1. These numbers include both positive and negative numbers.

2. These numbers can be located at a specific point on a number line.

3. Integers are included in this category.

4. Fractions belong in this category.

5. Decimals belong in this category.

6. Terminating decimals are found in this number group.

7. Nonrepeating decimals are part of this number group.

8. Repeating decimals are part of this number group.

9. These numbers are part of the real number system.

10. Pi (3.14) is an example.

11. Three-fifths is an example.

I just can't stand it. You're so irrational!

Rational Numbers		**Irrational Numbers**	
_____	_____	_____	_____
_____	_____	_____	_____
_____	_____	_____	_____
_____	_____	_____	_____
_____	_____	_____	_____
_____		_____	

Name _____ Date _____

EXERCISE 51: WRITING TO COMPARE (CONTINUED)

13. In the next exercise you will write and compare the rational and irrational numbers. You are going to tell how they are alike. You will need a topic sentence that introduces the paragraph. You may use one of your own topic sentences or select one of the following.

    The rational and irrational numbers are much alike.
    The rational and irrational numbers are very important in mathematics.
    The rational and irrational numbers are more alike than they are different.

Topic sentence:

_____

_____

Tell how the numbers are different:

_____

_____

_____

_____

_____

_____

_____

_____

_____

Concluding sentence:

_____

_____

Name _____ Date _____

EXERCISE 52: SIGNAL WORDS USED IN COMPARATIVE WRITING

You have learned in writing to contrast about signal words. The signal words in writing to contrast alerted people who read your writing that a difference was indicated. When writing to compare, signal words are used to alert the reader that things are alike. Signal words used in writing to compare are **likewise**, **similarly**, **as**, **also**, **additionally**, **furthermore**, and **besides**.

Example without signal word:
Rational numbers include fractions. Irrational numbers include fractions.

Example with signal word:
Rational numbers include fractions as irrational numbers do.

In this exercise you are to rewrite the comparison paragraph you wrote in Exercise 50 about rational and irrational numbers. Rewrite the paragraph and combine sentences using the signal words *likewise, similarly, as, also, additionally, furthermore, besides.*

You may want to change some of the original sentences to use a signal word, but it is not necessary that every sentence have a signal word.

_____
_____
_____
_____
_____
_____
_____
_____
_____
_____
_____

Name_____ Date_____

EXERCISE 53: WRITING A FRIENDLY LETTER

People often write letters to friends. Usually when writing a friend you write what is called a friendly letter. When writing a friendly letter, you will write a more interesting letter if you organize your thoughts before you write.

There are five main parts to develop in a friendly letter. The five parts are the heading, salutation(greeting), body, closing, and signature.

Heading: This is your address along with the date. Place the heading in the upper right-hand corner of the letter.

Address:
City/State/Zip:
Date:

123 West Third Street
Anytown, Arizona 11111
December 10, 1996

Salutation(greeting):
This is usually informal.

Dear Sarah,

Body of the letter:

Here you write to your friend.

Closing (a good-bye):
Your signature:

Your friend,
Emily

In the next exercise you are to write a friendly letter to a friend about the prime and composite numbers. You must also think of ways to make the letter interesting. One way to make the letter interesting is to compare or contrast the topics discussed. In preparing to write, review the statements under Prime Number Statements and Composite Number Statements in Exercise 49.

_____
_____
_____
_____
_____
_____
_____
_____
_____

Name _____ Date _____

Learning About Subjects and Predicates

In the following exercise you will learn about subjects and predicates. Word problems in mathematics have sentences. When solving word problems, it is important to be able to pick out key elements. In sentences, the subject and the predicate are the key elements. The subject in a sentence is the thing talked about. The predicate tells something about the subject.

Example subject: The natural numbers do not include zero.
The thing talked about is natural numbers. The phrase "The natural numbers" is the subject.

Example predicate: The natural numbers do not include zero.
The part of the sentence "do not include zero." is the predicate. This part of the sentence tells about the subject.

EXERCISE 54: IDENTIFYING SUBJECTS AND PREDICATES

In the following sentences draw one line beneath the subject and draw two lines beneath the predicate.

1. The natural numbers do not include zero.

2. The natural numbers do not include fractions.

3. The natural numbers do include positive whole numbers.

4. Whole numbers include the natural numbers and zero.

5. Integers include the whole numbers and the negative whole numbers.

6. Rational numbers can all be located on a number line.

7. Rational numbers include terminating and repeating decimals.

8. A circle has a diameter of four inches.

9. Six has the factors one, two, three, and six.

10. Three has the factors one and three.

I may not be natural, but at least I am a whole number.

Name _____ Date _____

EXERCISE 55: IDENTIFYING SUBJECTS AND PREDICATES IN WORD PROBLEMS

Mathematical problems often tell you to "find" something. For example: The diameter of a circle is four inches. Find the circumference.

In the first sentence, the subject is "The diameter." In the second sentence, the subject is "You", but it is not written. It is understood. In many math problems, the subject "You" is understood or is not stated.

Find the subject and predicate in each sentence in the following problems. Write the subject on the blank beside each problem.

1. Two to the second power is written as 2^2. _____

2. Write two to the third power. _____

3. Raise three to the second power. _____

4. Three to the second power is nine. _____

Each of the problems below has more than one sentence. Write the subject for each of the sentences on the blank following it.

5. John ordered 27 pictures. _____ The pictures are in packets of three. _____
Find how many packets John will receive. _____

6. Marie is lifting weights. _____ She has weights of 10 lbs., 20 lbs., and 25 lbs. _____
Find the average weight of the weights. _____

7. Sammy was sorting apples. _____ He found that 5 out of each 100 apples were rotten. ___
Find the percent of the apples that were rotten. _____

Each of the problems below has more than one sentence. Write the predicate for each of the sentences on the blank following it.

8. John ordered 27 pictures. _____
The pictures are in packets of three. _____
Find how many packets John will receive. _____

9. Marie is lifting weights. _____
She has weights of 10 lbs., 20 lbs., and 25 lbs. _____
Find the average weight of the weights. _____

10. Sammy was sorting apples. _____
He found that 5 out of each 100 apples were rotten. _____
Find the percent of the apples that were rotten. _____

Name _____ Date _____

EXERCISE 56: USING SUBJECTS AND PREDICATES TO WRITE ABOUT MATH

Write the observations you make about the following numbers: 7, 11, 17, 19, 32, 44, 57, 81. Observations are just statements about what you find as you work with numbers. Each observation is to be written with a subject and predicate.

Use the following to help guide your written observations.

Are the numbers all composite numbers?

Are the numbers all prime numbers?

Do the numbers all have factors?

If any numbers have factors, are the factors all the same?

What is different, if anything, about the factors for 19, 11, 7, 17 and 44, 57, 32, and 81?

What are possible classifications in which the numbers above can be placed?

Odd and even factors other than the number and one.

Odd and even numbers that can be factored.

Composite numbers that can be factored.

Prime numbers that cannot be factored.

You may have other observations. Write your observations on the blanks that follow. Make certain that each observation is written with a subject and predicate.

_____

_____

_____

_____

_____

_____

_____

_____

_____

_____

_____

_____

Name_____ Date_____

EXERCISE 57: NUMBER SYSTEM REVIEW

Fill in the blanks in the following selections using words from the lists found above each paragraph.

2^4 factors   odd   16   exponent   even   2, 2, 2, 2

I am an (1)_____ number with the (2)_____ 3, 1, and 5. My neighbor is the (3)_____ number (4)_____ , which has the factors (5)_____ . Since those factors are all the same number, they may be written with an (6)_____ as (7)_____ .

zero   whole   negative   positive   number

There are no (8)_____ numbers in my family. Anyone working with the numbers in my family will have a positive experience. Oh! Well, there is a member of the family that is neither a (9)_____ nor a negative (10)_____ . That member of the family is a (11)_____ . My family is called the (12)_____ numbers.

zero   positive   natural

My family is the oldest number family. Some of the family members tell me that the family might have developed to replace the sticks or stones shepherds were using to keep track of the animals. My family of numbers is called (13)_____ numbers. Unlike the whole number family, there isn't a (14)_____ in my family. Ours is a very (15)_____ family.

integers   fractions   negative   decimals

There are as many (16)_____ numbers as there are positive numbers in this family. There are no (17)_____ or (18)_____ in the family, so one might say we aren't fractured. Even though our family can't help divide a pie or cake into equal parts, we can tell you when the temperature is below zero. We are the (19)_____ .

rational   decimal   specific   repeating

Every member of our family can be located at a (20)_____ point on the number line. That may be one reason we are known as the (21)_____ numbers. The (22)_____ members of the family are either terminating or (23)_____ .

nonterminating   fractions   decimals   irrational   point   pi

In my family there are many (24)_____ and (25)_____ . All are (26)_____ , and these are not found at a specific (27)_____ on the number line. A most famous member of the family is 3.14, also known as (28)_____ . Even though the family is known as (29)_____ , we are very important.

Answer Keys

EXERCISE 1: REDUCE TO COMMON FRACTIONS (PAGE 2)

1. $\frac{1}{2}$ 2. $\frac{2}{3}$ 3. $\frac{1}{5}$ 4. $\frac{1}{4}$ 5. $\frac{2}{3}$ 6. $\frac{1}{4}$

7. $\frac{1}{2}$ 8. $\frac{3}{4}$ 9. $\frac{3}{8}$ 10. $\frac{3}{10}$ 11. $\frac{4}{5}$ 12. $\frac{3}{4}$

13. 1   14. $\frac{5}{7}$ 15. $\frac{5}{6}$

Rule to reduce to common fractions: Divide both terms of a fraction by the same number in order to reduce to a common fraction.

EXERCISE 2: ADDING OR SUBTRACTING FRACTIONS WITH THE SAME DENOMINATOR (PAGE 3)

1. $\frac{5}{6}$ 2. $\frac{7}{20}$ 3. $\frac{7}{12}$ 4. 1   5. $\frac{11}{12}$ 6. $\frac{35}{64}$

7. $\frac{3}{20}$ 8. 1   9. $\frac{4}{7}$ 10. $\frac{4}{9}$ 11. $\frac{9}{50}$ 12. $\frac{8}{25}$

Rule to Add or Subtract Fractions With the Same Denominator: When adding or subracting fractions that have the same denominator, add or subtract the numerators and keep the same denominator.

EXERCISE 3: ADDING OR SUBTRACTING FRACTIONS WITH DIFFERENT DENOMINATORS (PAGE 4)

1. $\frac{23}{30}$ 2. $\frac{11}{20}$ 3. $1\frac{13}{16}$ 4. $\frac{5}{8}$ 5. $1\frac{5}{36}$ 6. $\frac{2}{3}$

7. $\frac{1}{2}$ 8. $\frac{7}{8}$ 9. $\frac{11}{14}$ 10. $\frac{11}{18}$ 11. $\frac{13}{50}$ 12. $\frac{1}{10}$

Rule for Adding or Subtracting Fractions With Different Denominators: When adding or subtracting fractions with different denominators, find a common denominator, rewrite each fraction using the common denominator, and then add or subtract the numerators.

EXERCISE 4: MULTIPLYING FRACTIONS (PAGE 5)

1. $\frac{1}{12}$ 2. $\frac{3}{50}$ 3. $\frac{45}{64}$ 4. $\frac{3}{32}$ 5. $\frac{2}{9}$ 6. $\frac{5}{64}$

7. $\frac{7}{50}$ 8. $\frac{3}{32}$ 9. $\frac{15}{98}$ 10. $\frac{1}{24}$ 11. $\frac{17}{625}$ 12. $\frac{3}{25}$

Rule for Multiplying Fractions: Multiply the numerators to find the numerators of the answer and then multiply the denominators to find the denominators of the answer.

EXERCISE 5: MULTIPLYING A FRACTION AND A WHOLE NUMBER (PAGE 6)

1. $1\frac{1}{3}$ 2. $1\frac{1}{2}$ 3. $2\frac{1}{2}$ 4. 5   5. $3\frac{3}{4}$ 6. $70\frac{2}{3}$

7. $13\frac{1}{3}$ 8. $5\frac{2}{3}$ 9. $261\frac{2}{3}$ 10. $21\frac{1}{3}$ 11. 4   12. $717\frac{1}{2}$

Rule for Multiplying Fractions and Whole Numbers: To multiply a fraction by a whole number, multiply the numerator of the fraction by the whole number and then divide that product by the denominator and reduce the answer.

Exercise 6: Multiplying Fractions and Mixed Numbers (page 7)

1. $7\frac{1}{2}$ 2. $\frac{7}{9}$ 3. $4\frac{1}{2}$ 4. $4\frac{9}{16}$ 5. $30\frac{2}{5}$ 6. $7\frac{1}{24}$
7. $19\frac{9}{25}$ 8. $14\frac{2}{9}$ 9. $10\frac{9}{16}$ 10. $15\frac{1}{6}$ 11. $7\frac{33}{64}$ 12. $19\frac{1}{4}$

Rule for Multiplying Fractions and Mixed Numbers: When multiplying fractions and mixed numbers, write the mixed numbers as improper fractions and then multipy the fractions and reduce.

Exercise 7: Dividing Fractions (page 7)

1. $\frac{4}{21}$ 2. $\frac{2}{5}$ 3. $\frac{5}{6}$ 4. $1\frac{1}{2}$ 5. 1 6. $8\frac{2}{5}$
7. $\frac{25}{52}$ 8. $\frac{5}{6}$ 9. $2\frac{1}{4}$ 10. $\frac{3}{8}$ 11. $\frac{2}{5}$ 12. 9

Rule for Dividing Fractions: To divide a fraction, invert the divisor and multipy.

Exercise 8: Dividing Mixed Numbers or a Fraction by Whole Numbers (page 9)

1. $10\frac{10}{21}$ 2. 39 3. $1\frac{3}{22}$ 4. $2\frac{17}{20}$ 5. $9\frac{7}{12}$ 6. 16
7. 24 8. 162 9. $2\frac{233}{266}$ 10. 1 11. $35\frac{3}{5}$ 12. 12

Rule for Dividing Mixed Numbers or a Fraction by Whole Numbers : To divide a mixed number by a fraction, change the mixed number to an improper fraction, then invert the divisor and multiply.

Exercise 9: Expressing Common fractions as Decimals (page 10)

1. 0.5   2. 0.083   3. 0.583   4. 0.75   5. 0.6   6. 0.125
7. 0.67   8. 0.56   9. 0.25   10. 0.375   11. 0.3125   12. 0.22

Rule for Expressing Common Fractions as Decimals: In order to change a fraction to a decimal, divide the numerator by the denominator.

Exercise 10: Dividing Decimals and Placing the Decimal (page 11)

1. 20   2. 178.57   3. 1,325   4. 62.5   5. 1,000

Rule for Dividing Decimals and Placing the Decimal: To divide by a decimal, first change the divisor to a whole number by multipling the divisor and the dividend by 10; 100; 1,000; and so on and then dividing in the normal fashion.

Exercise 11: Multiplying and Placing the Decimal (page 12)

1. 0.081   2. 0.62   3. 72   4. 1.9437   5. 5.06   6. 1.15
7. 2.32   8. 0.0225

Rule for Multiplying and Placing the Decimal: The total number of places in a product is equal to the total number of decimal places in the two numbers that were multiplied.

Exercise 12: Multiplying and Dividing by 10, 100, and 1,000 (page 13)

1. 490	2. 36	3. 0.2	4. 980
5. 3,900	6. 230	7. 5	8. 8,900
9. 270	10. 5,900	11. 70	12. 27,000
13. 1.8	14. 0.69	15. 0.008	16. 1.3
17. 0.67	18. 0.071	19. 0.0005	20. 0.41
21. 0.087	22. 0.0043	23. 0.00009	24. 0.057

25. To multiply a decimal by 10, I moved the decimal point **one** places to the **right**.
26. To multiply a decimal by 100, I moved the decimal point **two** places to the **right**.
27. To multiply a decimal by 1000, I moved the decimal point **three** places to the **right**.
28. To divide a decimal by 10, I moved the decimal point **one** places to the **left**.
20. To divide a decimal by 100, I moved the decimal point **two** places to the **left**.
30. To divide a decimal by 1000, I moved the decimal point **three** places to the **left**.

Exercise 13: Solving an Equation When the Variable Is Multiplied by a Number (page 15)

1. 6	2. 3	3. 8	4. 8
5. 5	6. 4	7. 6	8. 5

Solving an Equation When the Variable Is Multiplied by a Number: If a variable in an equation is multiplied by a number, solve by dividing each side of the equation by that number.

Exercise 14: Solving an Equation When the Variable Is Divided by a Number (page 16)

1. 192	2. 2,304	3. 384	4. 0.24
5. 40.5	6. 1.764	7. 39.96	8. 1,089

Solving an equation when the variable is divided by a number: If a variable in an equation is divided by a number, solve by multiplying each side of the equation by that number.

Exercise 15: Using Inverse Operations (page 17)

1. Subtraction
2. Addition
3. Division
4. Multiplication

5. 34	6. 104	7. 2.67 or $2\frac{2}{3}$	8. 0.76

Exercise 16: Measuring the Perimeter and Area of Squares and Rectangles (pages 18–20)

1. 4 inches
2. 1 square inch
3. square inch
4. square foot
5. square yard
6. square millimeter
7. square centimeter
8. square decimeter
9. square meter
10. square mile
11. square hectare

85

12. To divide into two equal parts.
13. The square has been divided into four smaller squares.
14. 8 inches.
15. 4 square inches
16. 6 squares
17. 12 inches
18. 9 square inches
19. When you use a ruler or some other measuring device to measure an object.
20. Length x Width
   In order to find the area of a rectangle or square, you need to multiply the length of the figure by its width.

21. 16 sq. cm   22. 81 sq. mm   23. 156.25 sq. in.   24. 289 sq. yds.
25. 1.69 sq. ft.   26. 21.16 sq. mi. 27. 1082.41 sq. m   28. 349.69 sq. ft.
29. 8 sq. in.   30. 17 sq. in.   31. 16 sq. yds.
32. 168 sq. yds.   33. 10.8 sq. mm   34. 32.4 sq. yds.
35. 10.81 sq. mi. 36. 24 sq. cm

EXERCISE 17: FINDING THE PERIMETER AND AREA OF FIGURES (PAGE 21)

To figure the perimeters, simple addition will work. To figure the areas, there may be several acceptable answers. Only one explanation will be given here, however.

1. 40 yds.   2. 75 sq. yds.
There are two basic rectangles in this figure: 10 yds. x 5 yds. = 50 sq. yds.
                                             + 5 yds. x 5 yds. = 25 sq. yds.
                                                                 75 sq. yds.

3. 28 in.   4. 24 sq. in.
There are three basic rectangles in this figure: 7 in. x 2 in. = 14 sq. in.
                                                 2 in. x 2.5 in. = 5 sq. in.
                                               + 2 in. x 2.5 in. = 5 sq. in.
                                                                  24 sq. in.

5. 100 m   6. 561 sq. m
There are two basic rectangles in this figure:
          The outside figure: 25 meters x 25 meters = 625 sq. meters
          The inside figure: – 8 meters x 8 meters =   64 sq. meters
                                                         561 sq. meters

7. 180 ft.   8. 720 sq. ft.
There are four basic rectangles in this figure: 40 ft. x 10 ft. = 400 sq. ft.
                                                 10 ft. x 20 ft. = 200 sq. ft.
                                                  8 ft. x 10 ft. = 80 sq. ft.
                                               + 4 ft. x 10 ft. = 40 sq. ft.
                                                                   720 sq. ft.

EXERCISE 18: MEASURING THE AREA OF A TRIANGLE (PAGES 22–23)

1. Triangles 2. Equal 3. Yes 4. Yes 5. Rectangle 6. A = L x W
7. Since the area of two equal triangles is equal to the area of a rectangle, then the area of a triangle is equal to one half of the area of a rectangle.
8. $A = \frac{1}{2} b \times h$

EXERCISE 19: FINDING THE AREA OF A TRIANGLE (PAGE 24)

1. 6 ft., 3 ft.   2. 6 cm, 10 cm   3. 20 in., 12 in.
4. 17.5   5. 75   6. 3   7. 18.36
8. 95   9. 205.5   10. 113.52   11. 770
12. $\frac{7}{8}$ 13. 12 $\frac{3}{16}$ 14. 52 $\frac{1}{2}$ 15. 62 $\frac{11}{96}$
16. 9 $\frac{661}{864}$ 17. 7 $\frac{133}{162}$

EXERCISE 20: LEARNING MORE ABOUT TRIANGLES (PAGES 25–26)

1, 3, and 4 will have plus marks   5. Teacher check
6. 4   7. 2   8. 4   9. 1   10. 1   11. 1   12. 1
13. $\frac{1}{4}$ 14. $\frac{1}{4}$ 15. $\frac{1}{4}$ 16. $\frac{1}{4}$ 17. yes   18. yes
19–23 Teacher check   24. $\frac{1}{2}$ 25. $\frac{1}{4}$ 26. $\frac{1}{2}$ 27. $\frac{1}{4}$
28. $\frac{1}{2}$ 29. $\frac{1}{4}$

EXERCISE 21: MEASURING THE AREA OF A PARALLELOGRAM (PAGES 27–28)

1. A = L x W   2. A = $\frac{1}{2}$ b x h
3. Parallelogram: A plane figure with four sides, with the opposite sides parallel and equal.
4. 1, 2, 3, 5, 6
5. 4—Triangle, 7—Tapezoid, 8—Oval
6. Rectangle   7. Same   8. A = L x W   9. A = b x h
10. 48   11. 168   12. 4   13. 22.72
14. 151.8   15. 311.5   16. 191.7   17. 2,494
18. 3 $\frac{5}{9}$ 19. 17 $\frac{17}{32}$ 20. 298 $\frac{1}{2}$ 21. 168 $\frac{21}{32}$
22. 32 $\frac{4}{27}$ 23. 6 $\frac{109}{432}$

EXERCISE 22: MEASURING THE AREA OF A CIRCLE (PAGES 29–31)

1. Should be approximately 3.14.   2. π or pi.   3. Divide the circumference by π.
4. 1.91 cm   5. 5.41 in.   6. 10.19 m   7. 5.73 mm
8. 3.82 yds.   9. 7.47 ft.   10. 4.14 mi.   11. 99.62 m
12. Multiply the circumference by π.
13. 9.42 cm   14. 40.82 in.   15. 72.22 m   16. 37.68 mm
17. 28.26 yds.   18. 41.04 ft.   19. 668.82 mi.   20. 347.60 m
21. Multiply the radius by two and then multipy by π.
22. 12.56 cm   23. 175.84 in.   24. 45.22 m   25. 44.78 mm
26. 43.96 yds.   27. 107.2 ft.   28. 38.43 mi.   29. 777.46 m
30. d= c/π   31. c = πd   32. c = 2πr
33. 1,519.76 sq. cm   34. 19, 596.74 sq. in.
35. 530.66 sq. m   36. 1,661.06 sq. mm
37. 379.94 sq. yds.   38. 566.35 sq. ft.
39. 286.98 sq. mi.   40. 38,548.65 sq. m

EXERCISE 24: LEARNING MORE ABOUT CIRCLES (PAGES 32–33)

1a. 2   b. inches   2a. 1   b. inches
3a. 6.28   b. inches   4a. 3.14   b. square inches
5a. 8   b. inches   6a. 4   b. square inches
7–9. Teacher check   10–13. Either answer is acceptable.

14. Teacher check   15a. 4   b. inches   16a. 2   b. inches
17a. 39.44   b. square inches   18a. 12.56   b. inches
19. Teacher check   20a. 4   b. inches   21a. 16   b. inches
22a. 16   b. square inches   23. Teacher check

EXERCISE 25: FINDING THE AREA OF COMBINED PLANE FIGURES (PAGE 34)

1. Answer: 470.592 sq. in.
Explanation: Using **A = L x W** figure the area of the rectangle. Using **A = ½b x h** figure the areas of the two triangles. Add the three areas.
2. Answer: 289.125 sq. in.
Explanation: Using **A = L x W** figure the area of the rectangle. Using **A = πr²** figure the area of the circle that forms the ends of the figure (divide 15 by 2 to find the radius). Add the two areas.
3. Answer: 64.26 sq. in.
Explanation: Using **A = L x W** figure the area of the square. Using **A = πr²** figure the area of a circle with a radius of 6 inches, then divide that answer by 4, since only a fourth of circle is included in the figure. Add the two areas.
4. Answer: 597.1195 sq. in.
Explanation: Using **A = L x W** figure the area of the rectangle. Using **A = ½b x h** figure the area of the triangle. Using **A = πr²**, figure the area of a circle with a diameter of 23.75 in. (divide 23.75 by 2 to find the radius), and then divide that answer by 2, since only half a circle is included in the figure. Add the three areas.

EXERCISES 26–33
Teacher Check

EXERCISE 34: DETERMINING IF A NUMBER IS RATIONAL OR IRRATIONAL (PAGE 47)

Decimal Form	Repeating	Nonrepeating	Terminating	Rational	Irrational
1. 0.875			X	X	
2. 0.666667	X			X	
3. 0.285714286	X			X	
4. 0.833333	X			X	
5. 0.714285714	X			X	
6. 0.888889	X			X	
7. 0.5			X	X	
8. 0.785714286	X			X	
9. 0.941176471	X			X	
10. 0.954545455	X			X	
11. 1.414213562		X			X
12. 2.236067978		X			X
13. 4.123105626		X			X
14. 2.0			X	X	
15. 8.0			X	X	
16. 16.0			X	X	
17. 5.567764363		X			X
18. 9.0			X	X	
19. 11.0			X	X	
20. 7.745966692		X			X

EXERCISE 35: WHAT WOULD YOU DO? (PAGES 48-49)
Teacher check

EXERCISE 36: ORGANIZING PARAGRAPHS (PAGES 50–51)
Sentence order: 6, 3, 1, 4, 7, 5, 2
Teacher check paragraphs

EXERCISE 37: DESCRIPTIVE WRITING (PAGES 52–53)
Teacher check

EXERCISE 38: UNDERSTANDING AND USING MATHEMATIC SYMBOLS (PAGES 54–55)
Students may use these mathematical terms or other words of equivalent meaning.
1. minus
2. does not equal
3. divide
4. similar
5. add
6. pie; equal to or greater than
7. radical
8. set
9. subset; set
10. one to one
11. plus or minus
12. 46; 54
13. one to one; 50; one
14–17. Teacher check

EXERCISE 39: MATHEMATIC SYMBOLS CROSSWORD PUZZLE (PAGE 56)

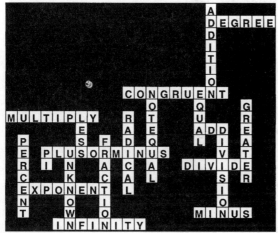

EXERCISE 40: WRITING ABOUT MATHEMATIC FORMULAS (PAGES 57–58)
Teacher check

EXERCISE 41: FINDING SQUARE ROOTS (PAGE 59)

1. 3	2. 4	3. 6	4. 9	5. 12
6. 11	7. 1	8. 2	9. 10	10. 7
11. 5	12. 8	13. 18	14. 25	15. 20

EXERCISE 42: SQUARE ROOT SENTENCES (PAGE 60)

Teacher check odd-numbered sentences.

2a. 100   b. 81   4a. 16   b. 4   6a. 1   b. 4   8a. 36   b. 64   10a. 81   b. 9

EXERCISE 43: DIALOGUE AMONG NUMBERS (PAGES 61–62)

Teacher check

EXERCISE 44: EXPONENT PROBLEMS AND DIALOGUE (PAGE 63)

1. 1	2. 4	3. 9	4. 16	5. 25	6. 36	7. 49
8. 1	9. 8	10. 27	11. 64	12. 125	13. 216	14. 343
15. 1	16. 16	17. 81	18. 256	19. 625	20. 1296	21. 2401

22. Teacher check

EXERCISE 45: LEARNING ABOUT BASE TWO (PAGES 64–65)

1. 1	2. 2	3. 4	4. 8	5. 16	6. 32
7. 3	8. 5	9. 6	10. 11		
11. 2^2	12. 2^3	13. 2^4	14. 2^5	15. 2^6	16. 2^7

17. a) 2^5 b) 2^4 c) 2^3 d) 2^2

18. a) 2^7 b) 2^6 c) 255 Base Ten

19. 34	20. 40	21. 17	22. 75	23. 61	24. 29	25. 130
26. 1111	27. 100011	28. 11010	29. 10100	30. 110010		

EXERCISE 46: LEARNING ABOUT BASE FIVE (PAGES 66–67)

1. "one, four, three, three"
2. "two, nine"
3. "two, two, one"
4. "one, three, two, one, one"
5. "two, four, three, one, three"

6. 1	7. 5	8. 25	9. 125	10. 625
11. 39	12. 371	13. 31	14. 105	15. 68
16. 5^2	17. 5^3	18. 5^4	19. 5^5	

20. a) 5^4 b) 5^3 c) 5^2 d) 5^1

21. 340	22. 20000	23. 11422	24. 13304	25. 133

EXERCISE 47: WRITING EXERCISE FOR NUMBER BASES (PAGE 68)

Teacher check

EXERCISE 48: FINDING FACTORS (PAGE 70)

1. 2, 2, 2, or 2^3
2. 3, 5
3. 5, 5, or 5^2
4. 5, 5, 2, 2 or 5^2, 2^2
5. 2, 2, 2, 2, or 2^4
6. 19, 1
7. 2, 2, 11 or 2^2, 11
8. 11, 1
9. 7, 1
10. 3, 3, or 3^2
11. 1, 31
12. 2, 2, 2, 2, 2, or 2^5
13. 3, 7
14. 2, 5, 5, or 2, 5^2
15. 2, 13
16. 2, 3, 13
17. 2, 5, 3, 3, or 2, 5, 3^2
18. 3, 3, 3, 3 or 3^4
19. 3, 19
20. 2, 7, 7 or 2, 7^2

EXERCISE 49: WRITING TO CONTRAST (PAGES 71–72)

Prime Number Statements: 1, 2, 5, 8, 10, 11
Composite Number Statements: 3, 4, 5, 6, 7, 9, 12
Teacher check paragraphs

EXERCISE 50: SIGNAL WORDS USED TO CONTRAST (PAGES 73–74)

Teacher check

EXERCISE 51: WRITING TO COMPARE (PAGES 75–76)

Rational Number Statements: 1, 2, 3, 4, 5, 6, 7, 8, 9, 11
Irrational Number Statements: 1, 5, 7, 9, 10
Teacher check paragraphs

EXERCISE 52: SIGNAL WORDS USED IN CAMPARATIVE WRITING (PAGE 77)

Teacher check

EXERCISE 53: WRITING A FRIENDLY LETTER (PAGE 78)

Teacher check

EXERCISE 54: IDENTIFYING SUBJECTS AND PREDICATES (PAGE 79)

1. The natural numbers do not include zero.
2. The natural numbers do not include fractions.
3. The natural numbers do include positive whole numbers.
4. Whole numbers include the natural numbers and zero.
5. Integers include the whole numbers and the negative whole numbers.
6. Rational numbers can all be located on a number line.
7. Rational numbers include terminating and repeating decimals.
8. A circle has a diameter of four inches.
9. Six has the factors one, two, three, and six.
10. Three has the factors one and three.

EXERCISE 55: IDENTIFYING SUBJECTS AND PREDICATES IN WORD PROBLEMS (PAGE 80)

1. Two
2. You
3. You
4. Three
5. John; The pictures; You
6. Marie; She; You
7. Sammy; He; You

8. ordered 27 pictures.;
are in packets of three.;
Find how many packets John will receive.
9. is lifting weights.;
has weights of 10 lbs., 20lbs., and 25lbs.;
Find the average weight of the weights.
10. was sorting apples.;
found that 5 out of each 100 apples were rotten.;
Find the percent of the apples that are rotten.

Exercise 56: Using Subjects and Predicates to Write About Math (page 81)
Teacher check

Exercise 57: Numbers Review (page 82)
1. odd   2. factors   3. even   4. 16   5. 2, 2, 2, 2   6. exponent   7. 2^4

8. negative   9. positive   10. number   11. zero   12. whole

13. natural   14. zero   15. positive

16. negative   17. fractions/decimals   18. decimals/fractions   19. integers

20. specific   21. rational   22. decimal   23. repeating

24. decimals/fractions   25. fractions/decimals   26. nonterminating   27. point
28. pi   29. irrational